1991

The Decision-Making Process in Journalism

W9-ABR-424

The Decision-Making Process in Journalism

Carl Hausman

Nelson-Hall Publishers |nh| Chicago

Cover Painting: *Day 4 Searching* by Jadwiga Dziduch. Oil, 1987.

LIBRARY OF CONGRESS CATALOGING-IN-PUBLICATION DATA

Hausman, Carl, 1953-
    The decision-making process in journalism / Carl D. Hausman, Jr.
      p. cm.
    Includes bibliographical references.
    ISBN 0-8304-1203-4
    1. Journalism—Decision making. 2. Journalism—Objectivity.
    3. Journalistic ethics. 4. Journalism—Social aspects. I. Title.
    PN4749.H35 1989
    070.4'0684—dc20   89-12933
                                                    CIP

Manufactured in the United States of America

10   9   8   7   6   5   4   3   2   1

∞   TM The paper used in this book meets the minimum requirements of American National Standard for Information Sciences—Permanence of Paper for Printed Library Materials, ANSI Z39.48-1984.

C O N T E N T S

The Decision-Making Process in Journalism

PREFACE

The practice of journalism involves many decisions, decisions which often are made under intense time pressure and are of great consequence to the parties involved. But while this decision-making is an ongoing process and is one of the key factors in journalistic competence, very little guidance in this area is given to young reporters.

Making good journalistic decisions is often thought to be a function of news judgment, an acquired skill based on experience. Learning from one's mistakes exclusively, though, can be a painful way of acquiring news judgment. This work provides guidance and information designed to help the reader gain a degree of judgment by learning from the experiences of others.

The Decision-Making Process in Journalism examines how experienced journalists made decisions regarding newsworthiness, accuracy, fairness, logic, freedom from distortion, liability for libel or invasion of privacy, ethical professional practice, and the possible consequences of the story.

The work is written in the form of a handbook for the working journalist. Each chapter features discussion of the relevant issue, examples of how the principles are applied, and a combination of checklist/list of recommendations for evaluating a story or fact.

Material for *The Decision-Making Process in Journalism* is drawn from interviews with veteran journalists, research publications, journalism texts, and some cross-disciplinary sources, such as works on historiography and formal logic. Where appropriate, the author has also drawn on his own experience as a television anchor, reporter, talk show host, newspaper and magazine feature writer, and nonfiction book author.

CHAPTER 1

๛๛๛๛๛๛๛๛๛๛๛๛๛๛๛๛๛๛๛๛๛๛๛๛

Decisions in Modern Journalism

- You receive a call from a source who claims that a local politician is about to be indicted on fraud charges. There is little time to check the story out, and even if time were available, you know from experience that it is generally very difficult to get confirmation of pending indictments.

  Would you run the story?

- After a tragic fire, the chief of police tells you during an interview that four occupants of the apartment building died because there were no smoke detectors.

  Does this make sense—sense enough for you to print or broadcast the chief's conclusion?

- A state senator's son is arrested for possession of a small amount of marijuana. His father is a vigorous proponent of stiff antidrug laws.

  Do you run the story of the son's arrest, even though you would not normally use such a small possession story?

- You receive a press release which states that a study has concluded that insurance premiums in your state are fair and equitable. The press release is from the "Citizens' Center for Insurance Research."

  Do you use the press release?

Your answer to the above questions might be "it depends." And that, of course, is exactly the right answer. Decisions in journalism depend on a variety of factors—a mixture of intuition,

---

experience, and skepticism that veterans often like to call "news judgment."[1]

How Decisions Are Made

An experienced journalist, for example, would probably run the politician's indictment story if the reporter:

- knew the source, and knew him or her to be credible
- knew that the source indeed has access to the information
- knew, or at least strongly believed, that the source had no particular reason to falsify the information in order to damage the politician's reputation
- knew that the politician was capable of being involved in the activities for which he was being indicted

This was a real case,[2] and those criteria were met, *and* the story proved to be true, although bringing it to the attention of the public proved to be more difficult than at first imagined. (What actually happened is covered in detail in a later chapter.)

Sometimes, journalistic decisions depend on the analytical ability of the reporter or editor. Running a story which concludes that "four people died because there were no smoke detectors in the building" is a bad decision; it draws a conclusion not warranted by the facts. An unattended infant, for example, could not respond to a smoke detector and would likely have died regardless of the presence of the alarm. The fact that the story *sounds* logical—that it carries an enticing but incorrect linkage

---

1. The categories of decisions were determined through a variety of formal and informal interviews, including Davis (1987), Packard (1987), Petrow (1987), Schulte (1987), and Whearley (1987). Many of the categories were culled from examination of standard works in journalism, including Bittner & Bittner (1977), Gibson (1979), Metzler (1986), White, Meppen & Young (1984), plus many journal articles cited elsewhere.

2. From interview with Petrow (1987).

of cause and effect—brings the reporter into dangerous ethical and legal territory.[3]

The decision-making process often involves evaluation of the balance between an individual's right to privacy and the public's right and need to know. In the case of the politician's marijuana-smoking son, the young man might be deemed to have been thrust into the public light by virtue of his father's political stand on the drug issue. A panel of television news directors faced with this hypothetical dilemma during an ethics conference was unanimous in the contention that the public has a right to know about the fact that a vehemently antidrug public official's son uses marijuana. But what if the senator had not made drug use an issue in his campaign? Would the news directors use the story? Probably not, but—to bring up the salient point again—"it depends" on other related hypothetical factors.

On what would your decision about the hypothetical press release depend? Primarily on your knowledge of the "Citizens' Center for Insurance Research." Is it connected to a university? That would be a plus for the veracity of the information, though not necessarily a guarantee of its impartiality. Is this center funded by insurance companies? If so, the information is highly suspect.

The Necessary Skills

How does a journalist go about developing the skills necessary to pick his or her way through the minefield of journalistic decisions? Experience is the best teacher, but experience can also be a cruel taskmaster. Bad calls can damage peoples' reputations and, of course, reporters' careers. And although decision-making is an everyday, continuing process in all aspects of journalism, very little specific guidance is typically given to aspiring reporters as to the process of making decisions.

In addition, existing resources often are not helpful, or at least are not structured in a way that an inexperienced journalist can

---

3. Originally cited by the author in O'Donnell, Hausman & Benoit (1987), p. 165.

use them in the decision-making process. Former CBS News President Fred Friendly,[4] now a professor of journalism at Columbia University, summed up the situation when asked about the way he made decisions.

"Is there a book on television ethics? It probably isn't any good, because ethics involves so many things . . . so many decisions." Friendly, who indicated that those decisions are often made at the gut level, also pointed out that the inherent difficulty in deciding what's right is multiplied when the choice must be made under the intense time pressures of journalism.

Given these constraints, it is reasonable to assume that the newcomer to journalism needs general principles and guidelines for thinking through a problem—not detailed analyses of ethics and extended discussions of every permutation of a journalistic decision.

It is worth noting, incidentally, that journalistic decisions do not always involve purely ethical quandaries. Often, a reporter or editor is faced with a decision involving a procedural matter, such as how much weight to give to a particular witness's description of an event, or how much "play" should be allotted to a certain story during a newscast or in the makeup of a page of newsprint.

Another point: Decisions are not always the province of editors and news directors. Reporters often must make a series of snap decisions in the field, without benefit of editorial consultation. In short, decision-making extends beyond the realms of ethics or editing.

The process, of course, is not foolproof. Reporters and news executives frequently differ, sometimes bitterly, over the correctness of decisions. There is no journalistic component of, for example, the supposed mathematical precision of decision analysis in political science, where factors are weighted and mathematical formulae purport to identify the correct decision.

Instead, journalistic decisions are often based on what the reporter feels—by instinct and training—is right. Such decisions typically fall into the following categories:

---

4. Statement made during a symposium, 1987.

News Value

What makes news? Why, for example, is the arrest of the senator's son a story when a similar bust of an obscure perpetrator is not? The reason is tied to what journalists call "news value"— a nebulous but critical concept. There is a growing body of formal research describing the types of news items which gain coverage, but the research is clearly not definitive. In some cases, the concept of news value does become more clear when a reporter or editor is exposed to editorial conferences where each story is weighed and evaluated.[5] A combination of the two approaches—formal and observational—is presented in chapter 2: "Is It a Story?"

Truth and Reliability

Truth is not always a clearly defined issue. Is a press release from a partisan group, such as an insurance-industry controlled research organization, "true"? The figures may indeed be true, and there may be no direct misrepresentation of facts, but clearly the interpretation and presentation can be misleading and, under a certain set of definitions, untrue.

Journalists and historians are often called on to judge the veracity of statements of documents; this process is outlined in chapter 3: "Is It True?"

Fairness

Fairness, like truth, is a difficult concept to define with precision, and determining whether news coverage is fair is often a matter of experience and convention. In many cases, fairness involves questions of when and how to get the "other side" of the story—a practice complicated by the fact that there is virtually an infinite number of "sides" to any news item.

Completeness is an adjunct of fairness and is one of the most difficult concepts for a working journalist. Have enough people been asked for comment? Are there any unanswered questions?

---

5. For a re-creation of an editorial conference, see Adler (1971), pp. 127–131.

How many more calls must be made before the issue is covered? Those questions are dealt with in chapter 4: "Is It Fair?"

Logic

Journalistic blunders often are a result of a reporter jumping from point A to point Z without benefit of the rest of the alphabet—in other words, coming to conclusions not warranted by the facts. The smoke detector example given in the introduction to this chapter is one example of pseudo-logic at work. Confusion over cause and effect linkage is a common logical fallacy.

While formal logic is beyond the scope of newsroom operations, journalistic decisions are commonly based on logical inference and deduction. In addition, the increasing importance of statistics and statistical reasoning plays a major role in the journalist's job of interpreting information.

Both logical and statistical interpretation are examined in chapter 5: "Is It Logical?"

Distortion

Decisions relating to the structure of a story often center on whether or not the story was in some way distorted. Television, for example, is a medium of pictures, and in many cases a story will not be run if it does not contain pictures, especially *good* pictures.

Problems can and do arise from such visual requirements. As an example, when a television reporter arrives on the scene of a labor action at a time when there are no pickets, does he or she change the news by causing—directly or indirectly—the pickets to take the line again?

Distortion is not unique to the electronic media. Any print journalist realizes that good quotes will make the story more evocative. But do good quotes make good news? Does the powerful, catchy quote distort the true meaning of the story? And what about so-called "composite quotes," quotations invented from a melding of what several people said?

These and other issues are examined in chapter 6: "Is It Distorted?"

Decisions in Modern Journalism

Legalities

Recent research has show that fear of legal retribution has a considerable impact on how reporters go about their work. It seems quite clear that reporters and editors can become gun-shy because of the recent spate of libel and privacy cases.

Whether a story is legally actionable is a critical decision for a reporter, editor, or news director, and that decision is often made with little real understanding of what types of stories are dangerous and what elements must be present to constitute a libelous story or an invasion of privacy. Those and other details are discussed in chapter 7: "Is It Libelous or an Invasion of Privacy?"

Ethics

Ethics are a difficult set of rules to grasp, and written codes of ethics, while helpful, do not provide answers to all (and some would say most) problems encountered by journalists. That is why an examination of how experienced journalists go about testing their ethics is valuable.

Chapter 8: "Has the Story Been Ethically Researched and Presented?" seeks to synthesize the current body of thought on such issues as misrepresentation and using material from anonymous sources.

Consequences

Experienced journalists realize that many stories will involve someone being hurt or embarrassed. Being human, journalists weigh the likely benefits of the story against the possible negative results.

Such difficult decisions are discussed in chapter 9: "Is It Worth the Consequences?"

The Structure of This Book

The Decision-Making Process in Journalism is meant to be a working guide, and as such the verbiage is spare and the ideas presented simply but, it is hoped, not simplistically. There is often a temptation in a work of this nature to provide "cookbook" formulae; that, of course, is exactly the opposite of the author's intent. This book was written to give an insight into the thinking process of experienced journalists who have worked their way through problems of news judgment.

As a balancing mechanism, the first portion of the chapter provides a brief discussion of some of the concepts and issues involved in working through a particular type of journalistic decision: case histories, examples, and, where available, research results are examined. The second portion of the chapter shows some applications of the principles, and the third section presents a checklist of items to consider when evaluating a news judgment.

Before moving on to these chapters, though, remember a point which is critical to the use of this book: While there are right decisions and wrong decisions, a great many decisions fall into a twilight zone of sorts, where the issues are indistinct and the blacks and whites meld into maddening shades of grey. That, of course, comes with the territory. If journalistic decisions were clear-cut, there would be no need for editors, policy guidelines, editorial conferences, experience, and, of course, this book.

CHAPTER 2

᭦᭦᭦᭦᭦᭦᭦᭦᭦᭦᭦᭦᭦᭦᭦᭦᭦᭦᭦᭦᭦᭦

Is It News?

The question of what constitutes news stirs lively debate among novices and veterans alike. In actuality, no one has come up with an unchallenged definition of news, although not for want of trying.

"Everyone has a definition of what news is," notes Michael Short, Boston bureau chief of the Associated Press. "Most of the definitions are jokes: 'News is the same thing happening to different people,' or, 'News is what the editor thinks is news.' "[1]

And indeed, those are not terribly inaccurate characterizations of the basic idea. By news being "the same thing happening to different people," Short means that there are very few new occurrences in the news business. Murders, fires, business closings, and auto accidents happen with unfortunate regularity, but claim a different set of victims each time.

By characterizing news as "what the editor thinks is news," Short indicates that an editor or news director has a wide range of material from which to choose. Events won't become news until a news executive puts them in a newscast, newspaper, magazine, or book.

How Journalists Recognize News

The process of defining what is and what is not news is often a highly personal affair. Veteran journalists sometimes define news as "what I'm interested in." On close examination, that

---

1. Examples supplied by Short (1987).

definition makes as much sense as any, since experienced journalists make their livings by exploring items which interest the
readers or viewers who follow the journalist's work.

Author Vance Packard noted that his personal curiosity about
the restlessness and rootlessness of the people who moved in and
out of his New Canaan, Connecticut, neighborhood prompted
him to begin research for his book, *A Nation of Strangers.* "I got
tired of having to meet new neighbors," Packard said, "and I
began to wonder why all these people were coming and going."
Packard's curiosity evolved into a broad and insightful book
which climbed to sixth place on the *New York Times* bestseller
list—despite the fact that the work was based on a relatively
abstract idea. "It wasn't really a natural good book." Packard
noted, "but I think it was the best book I did."[2]

Perhaps journalists create news by propogating interest in what
interests them; or perhaps they simply reflect the tastes and
expectations of their viewers, listeners, and readers. In either
event, though, they do produce what we take to be news. It seems
safe to conclude, then, that the first definition of news is that
it is a story which includes some nugget of information that
intrigues people.

That nugget may be presented in the wrapping of either hard
or soft news. Hard news is traditionally taken to mean breaking
news, something out-of-the-ordinary that is happening currently
or happened recently, such as a fire. Note that the definition of
hard, breaking news intrinsically implies the concept of
timeliness. A fire which happened two months ago would be of
small interest to the public unless something new has recently
developed, perhaps in the investigation of the fire.

Soft news is usually thought of as feature news, news with a
bent of *human interest.* Human interest brings us back to the
apparently circular reasoning involved in determining what's
news ("news is what interests humans"), but closer examination
makes it apparent that what we really mean is that we're
interested in news that reflects "the human condition." The
human condition is that state of being long exploited by novelists
and playwrights, the idea that each of us longs to know that we

---

2. Packard (1987).

are not alone with our feelings and emotions—that others have the same hopes, doubts and worries as do we. For example, it is not by accident that so many novels and plays deal with the joy and pain of love. This is a topic of broad interest because readers and playgoers are gratified to see fictional characters (who reflect the human condition and experience) going though problems similar to those of the audience. Does it come as any surprise, then, that the feature pages of newspapers are filled with pieces on human relationships, such as divorce, dating, and preserving a happy marriage? Or that one staple of feature TV news is an investigation into the local singles' scene?

Stories dealing with comfort and security are part of the human condition, too. Witness journalists' preoccupation with financial stories. It is safe to assume that almost everyone is concerned to some degree with money and that this aspect of the human condition crosses over into both hard and soft news. Feature stories on earning and saving money dominate many feature pages in publications and are the subject of literally tens of thousands of published books. But anything which will likely affect a news consumer's pocketbook—such as a stock market gyration or change in the tax rate—is immediately a legitimate hard news item.

In summary, the first step in deciding what's news is to assess whether it has any immediate effect on readers, viewers, or listeners—whether, for example, it tugs at their heartstrings, their pocketbooks, or, in the case of actions of civil unrest or war, their desires for safety and stability.

Applications: How the Decisions Are Made

Journalists apply their knowledge of the human condition, and their concomitant knowledge of what interests news consumers, to determine what stories will be covered and featured. At newspapers, those determinations are often made in editorial conferences, where various departmental heads, known as sub-editors, "pitch" their ideas to the managing editor. The managing editor must then determine how closely each story fits his or her definition of news.

Each journalist has a different definition of news, but for the sake of discussion, here is one of the better definitions, presented by University of Oregon journalism professor Ken Metzler:

> News is prompt, "bottom line" recounting of factual information about events, situations, and ideas (including opinions and interpretations) calculated to interest an audience and help people cope with themselves and their environment.[3]

The typical day's menu of news items would certainly reflect many of the elements present in the above definition. The story of a blazing fire now burning in a downtown factory satisfies our need for prompt information about out-of-the-ordinary events. The column about rising mortgage rates fulfills our need for help in coping with our environment. The feature story on ways to stick to our diet through the holidays is an obvious attempt to help us cope with ourselves.

On a local and national level, it is apparent that those who report the news have developed a fairly clear set of expectations as to what they believe the public perceives as news. A study[4] undertaken of 180 days' worth of network newscasts, for example, showed that there is little real difference in the ways the three major commercial networks selected news; in other words, the producers of the programs possessed virtually identical news judgment. Interestingly, another study comparing on a day-to-day basis the lead stories in network TV newscasts found a striking similiarity in the stories elevated to lead status (run as the first story in the newscast).

It seems clear that this phenomenon, known as *consonance*, extends to the local media as well. A strong similarity of content was found in a study[5] comparing story selection among local stations in Detroit, Michigan, Toledo, Ohio, and Lansing,

---

3. Metzler (1987), p. 23.

4. The study conducted by Rife et al. (1986) examined random samples of 180 dates from Vanderbilt Television News Abstracts.

5. The study was conducted by Atwater (1986).

Michigan. In each case, an analysis of each market's newscasts indicated that about half the local news was duplicated by other stations in the market.

What does this mean for the emerging journalism professional? Essentially, these and other studies indicate that there is a reasonably clear standard of what is and what is not news. It is not a game without rules, and it is not nearly as mysterious a game as the newcomer might imagine. The studies of consonance and the empirical observations of journalists indicate that there actually are reasonably clear, if not completely defined, criteria for deciding what constitutes news.

Criteria: Is It News?

Here are some guidelines for making that determination. They are, of course, not definitive or all-inclusive, nor do they necessarily reflect an order of importance. The categories will, however, provide some basis for judging whether the particular event is, indeed, a news story.

1. Do many of your readers, listeners, or viewers identify with the subject, directly or indirectly? Direct identification might be exemplified by a sharp increase in new car prices, because readers or viewers may be forced to reconsider purchasing a new car. An indirect identification might be typefied by a fire in a downtown landmark building. Because many people are familiar with the building, the story will have more news value than would a fire in an isolated, rural area. Identification with the subject is why a story about the divorce of a movie star is news, even though most divorces generate little interest except to the parties involved. Identification is also why local events are generally of more interest than those which occur at a greater geographical distance.

2. Does the subject have an immediate and direct impact on news consumers? A story about food additives may have little news value to readers, viewers, or listeners in your area, but if the facts indicate that:

- the additive is used extensively in local meat-packing plants
- the additive can cause potentially fatal allergic reactions in some people

. . .the story assumes much greater news value.

The same argument for immediate and direct impact applies to stories dealing with taxes, municipal services, and to a certain extent, the story cited above concerning automobile prices.

3. Is the subject unusual? The "man bites dog" bromide holds a kernel of truth. Highly unusual occurrences do have news value entirely because of their unique nature. A widely publicized story about the romance of a New England moose and a dairy cow, for example, could have no conceivable impact on any human being except perhaps the owner of the cow. But it received national play entirely because of its rather strange nature.

On a more serious level, airplane crashes assume importance because it is still highly unusual for a vehicle to drop from the sky. The death of one person in a private plane crash is far more likely to make the news than the death of an automobile driver. Floods, forest fires, and other natural disasters also assume a level of importance due to their unusual nature. (They are obviously important news items for other reasons as well.)

4. Is the story timely? We tend to place a great importance, perhaps an exaggerated importance, on the newness of information. "Did you hear the latest?" is more than just a common figure of speech; it is a clear indication of our deep-seated desire to be among the first to receive information. Quite simply, new news is better news than old news.

5. Does the story have dramatic elements? The same factors which made a movie or book hold our interest pertain to news value as well. The story of a child trapped in a well (embodied in several famous news stories of this century) has a strong element of dramatic suspense: Will rescuers reach the child in time? The clash of two powerful politicians over the fate of a bill clearly offers the same kind of conflict as do fictional portrayals of conflict between and among powerful people.

6. Does the story involve great magnitude? The weight of

numbers is a strong determinant in the news value of a story. If a great many people die, it is more of a story; if a great deal of money is spent, the story assumes an elevated importance. And if an event occurs that potentially could affect or involve many people—such as an act which might provoke war— magnitude remains a factor that gives the story importance.

Case History: The Deadly Drive Home

The following case history dealt, in part, with things so commonplace that they're hardly noticed: guardrails, bridges, and traffic lights. But even though most of us don't think of these ubiquitous objects as being news, they certainly were part of a larger story—a story which won a duPont-Columbia award for WJXT Television in Jacksonville, Florida. The documentary, titled "The Deadly Drive Home," examined some of the factors which contributed to the high rate of traffic deaths in the area.

How did WJXT recognize the news value in something which might seem, at first, to be pretty routine? News Director Mel Martin and

2.1   Left to right: Mel Martin, Nancy Shafran, Tom Brokaw, and Bernard Shaw, Jan. 28, 1988, Alfred I. DuPont-Columbia University Awards.

The Decision-Making Process in Journalism

Assistant News Director Nancy Shafran developed the idea, and she explains it in this way: "Every few days the police would call us with another traffic fatality and give us the routine information. But when we began to look more closely, there were some things the police reports did *not* reveal. For example, the official report would say, 'Car A hit Car B.' But the people in Car B didn't die because Car A hit them; they died because Car B hit a telephone pole."

Why was that pole there? Why do we overlook other roadside hazards, such as guardrails, bridge supports, poorly placed trees, and even mailboxes—objects which are involved in almost ten thousand fatal collisions per year?

Some of the questions are answered in the following extract from "The Deadly Drive Home." Note how many of the points in the Is It News? checklist are reflected in the story. In particular, notice how viewers can readily identify with the subject, directly or indirectly. After all, most people who drive autos pass by these purported hazards on a daily basis. Think, too, of the number of people you *personally* know who have been injured in exactly the ways described in the following extract from the documentary.

No matter how hard anyone tries, the bad driving habits of many motorists are never going to be eliminated. There are also wrecks in which no driver is at fault; your tire blows out or you swerve to avoid hitting a child darting into the street. There are many other things that are beyond the drivers' control. They, too, can be killers:

About 1:30 New Year's morning, Jamie Mickler and Alan Greenwood of Mandarin were racing to a hospital. They wanted to be with a friend who had just been injured in an automobile accident.

Loretto Road was wet from the rain. Suddenly, Jamie lost control. His truck slid along the shoulder, knocked down a mail box, flipped on its side, and smashed into a JEA power pole.

Jamie and Alan, both 19 years old, became the first traffic fatalities of 1986.

In any accident, there are always a number of causes. The patrolman's report on this one said "careless" driving.

The families have said a lot of "what if's" . . . including

Excerpt from "The Deadly Drive Home" courtesy WJXT Television.

questions about the power pole located just a few feet from the road.

Charlie Greenwood is Alan's father:

"It was an accident, but still the concrete pole definitely stopped them dead. If it wasn't concrete and wasn't there, our boys might be."

Utility poles are just one of a long list of roadside hazards that we all drive by every day and never think about.

But each year ten thousand Americans die from collisions with trees, poles, guard rails, bridge supports, and even mail boxes.

At least 100,000 more people are injured. The cost of those accidents in dollars is believed to run into the billions.

This annual toll is nothing new.

The Insurance Institute for Highway Safety, using this film, pointed out the dangers of highway obstacles more than a decade ago.

But Florida must not have been paying attention. An estimated one-fifth to one-fourth of our highway deaths are linked to what safety experts call roadside booby-traps.

This collision with a utility pole in St. Augustine back in March claimed the life of a 62-year-old woman.

"There's a hierarchy of treament you can apply to any safety hazard."

Gerry Donaldson, an auto safety expert from Washington, D.C., found our roads littered with these booby-traps.

We brought Gerry here for two days earlier this month to make an inspection.

On I-95, driving south from the airport, he made his first discovery:

What did you see there?

"They left the concrete base at that grade that's poured in place for the sign support sitting out on the edge of the gore area. That's an incredible hazard."

It was a sign that had either fallen or been knocked down in the triangle (called a "gore area") that was formed where Hecksher Drive exits from the interstate.

The sign's 250 pound concrete base was lying in the dirt . . . and facing right out onto the highway.

What I'd like you to do is tell me how a car would end up hitting this thing.

"Easy. A car will be on the main line traffic . . . and he thinks he's going to continue. At the last minute for various reasons . . . he doesn't see the exit here, or he doesn't think its the proper exit and he will try to negotiate a last minute manuever . . . and especially at night and/or under inclement weather conditions, he'll come across here and he'll strike this sign."

A state highway crew should have either replanted the sign or hauled it away. "Here is an instance where a hazard has been created by completely unconscionable maintenance practices."

Design and construction practices are not much better, Donaldson noted.

He only had to look a few feet to find an even worse hazard. A concrete pillar dangerously close to the roadway with no guard rail to keep 55 mile per hour motorists away from it. He had a theory why highway officials have allowed it to be out there for years:

"They allowed prima facie hazardous conditions to prevail for a very long time on the notion that eventually they are going to be cured when available money and manpower come into play to be able to correct them . . . and in the nonce, you have many, many people lose their lives or suffer crippling, debilitating injuries."

Donaldson is the Director of Highway Safety for the Washington based Center for Auto Safety, a nonprofit research organization. As a nationally recognized authority, he has testified before Congress on vehicle and highway design. We brought him to Jacksonville to get his opinion on the roads our transportation planners are so proud of. First, we traveled Hecksher Drive where Donaldson found the bridges deplorable. He particularly criticized the railings—supposed safety devices—that he said don't amount to much more than decoration:

"It's basically nothing more than a fence that's been made of concrete. There was no thought about what happens if a vehicle contacted it and hit it."

You can also find on our highways' guard rails that are even less than fences. Take this one, for example, on the northbound lane of I-95 as you approach downtown:

"You might as well have a line of spaghetti down here on the side of the road . . . it's at least 14 to 16 inches below what it should be. It should be about 27 to 31 inches high, Tom. Any car is going to vault this and is going to go right over the roadside."

Is It News?

And why is this guard rail too low to do any good? Well, it appears that support posts have simply sunk into the ground.

But as a roadside hazard, this is nothing compared to what's right over there.

Our safety expert describes it as one of the most lethal booby-traps on any highway, anywhere.

This is the so-called gore area, the triangular space on I-95, where the highway splits . . . traffic to the right goes downtown, traffic to the left heads to the Fuller Warren . . . and in this vulnerable spot, the State of Florida has put up a huge overhead sign on a solid steel support that sits on a raised concrete pedestal. Then there's a blunt-end guard rail that would never deflect a direct hit from a car going the speed limit or slightly faster.

"The car will be totally demolished. The engine block will be pushed through the fire wall. The occupant will suffer overwhelmingly massive head and upper torso crush. He will have his femur, his thigh bones driven up through the pelvis into the chest cavity. It will be instant death."

Just looking at the banged-up metal here, it's obvious this place has a lurid history of encounters with cars:

Why on earth would anybody put guard rails here that are inadequate to protect this thing? Why would they do that?

"Because the management of your highway authority did not understand the function or the purpose of what guard rails are supposed to do . . . when they were originally installed, they were put there as a completely gratuitous feature of the highway. No more, no less than even some of the landscaping you may have there."

We took Donaldson's complaints about this section of 95 to the highway department's operations director, Grady Green:

"What you're saying is essentially correct. We must remember though [that what] was state of the art 25 or 30 years ago when these roads were designed and built for the increase in traffic and increased knowledge in the state of the art, we recognize that they are sub-standard today and as a matter of fact, the department recognized this some 10-12 years ago."

So for 10 to 12 years with traffic getting heavier all the time . . . drivers have had to endure this instrument of death and the State has known about it. Just look at that blunt end.

Here's what would happen if your car hit it at 55 miles per hour, a crash that would be similar to driving head first into a spear. But a blunt end is not necessary. The guard rail could have been flared and anchored in the ground at little expense, and we'd have one less hazard on the highway.

Despite that simple solution, the State says the reason nothing has been done is a lack of money. But money may not be the issue since the State is spending tax dollars to put back the same out-dated guard rail, the design that can kill and maim, the one Grady Green said was designed 25 to 30 years ago. Repeated accidents have bashed it beyond repair.

One day after we visited this spot, a construction crew, just by coincidence, came out to install a new version of the old guard rail complete with what workmen called a bull-nose. Donaldson would call it a battering ram aimed at on-coming cars. It makes you wonder what the guard rail is really there for.

The construction foreman, Terrance Hardiman, gave Rob Sweeting an answer:

"This is just to protect the sign structure, right here . . . that's what it is . . . just a bull-nose that is wrapped around that end."

And it's O.K. if cars run into the rail as long as they don't hit the sign structure.

"Yeah, I guess that's the way it looks, yeah, that's all it is. To protect that right there is really what it is."

There are better ways, safety systems which will cushion a collision and save a motorist from death or injury. Among them, an arrangement of plastic barrels containing sand. You see those barrels other places in Jacksonville. Why not at this 95 gore area?:

"Well, I don't know. We're fixing to overhaul that road right now in the next few months. Our maintenance generally is to maintain the facility as it was designed."

But keeping something as it was a quarter of a century ago doesn't seem to make sense when there are easier and better ways today.

The technology has existed for years to make our roadsides safer, but precious little of that technology can be found in the Jacksonville area. For example, signs that harmlessly break away when hit by a car are few and far between here.

By contrast, many of our intersections are loaded with lethal obstructions.

Traffic exiting from I-10 onto Roosevelt Blvd. encounters an array of potential killers where the highway crosses McDuff. A road sign held up by a 12-inch pipe is only about 2 feet from the street. Billboards sitting on other immovable metal posts are also close to oncoming cars, which are going about 40 miles an hour. And the traffic light. It is suspended from a pillar that is about a foot and a half wide, made out of solid concrete, and just inches from the road.

What is the reason for having such a gigantic concrete thing to hold up a traffic light?

"Tom, that's what it takes to hold it up; using the concrete poles, of course, is a maintenance free situation."

You, as a state employee, think of maintenance difficulties, but me, as a motorist, I worry about what is going to happen to me if I bump into that thing at 40 miles an hour.

"I was wondering why it doesn't have a slip base on it, the pole there, so if he hits it at 40-45 miles an hour . . . he doesn't have instantaneous deceleration on a concrete pole. It's good for not bringing down signalization systems, but it sure isn't good for the motorists."

"Tom, there's no question about it. If you impact the concrete pole you've got a problem on your hands."

"This is an incredibly lethal sight out here and it's just an instructive lesson on how public authorities care not at all for public safety. They only care about the convenience or the durability of their traffic control systems."

Of all the roadside hazards, the most prevalent, of course, are utility poles. Most of us simply assume telephone poles and JEA poles are just a fact of life that must be placed along the public right of way.

"Well, they don't have to be here and they are the second leading cause of death in the United States, Tom, for fixed object hazards."

The number-one roadside killer is trees. Some would say developers in Jacksonville have sharply reduced that problem here. Nevertheless, you will find palm trees planted years ago in the median strips of some of our older thoroughfares. Utility poles, on the other hand, are everywhere . . . and if you look at many of them, up close, you'll see the battle scars.

Southern Bell says it knows of 34 times last year phone poles needed to be replaced because they'd been hit. The JEA says so far this year 51 of its poles have been banged up. The authority's records indicate those accidents involved 29 injuries and one death. But, the JEA only keeps files on those wrecks in which its poles are damaged enough to require repair. The deaths of Jamie Mickler and Alan Greenwood New Year's morning at the JEA pole in Mandarin are not in the authority's records. That pole, and thousands more, are only a few feet and sometimes just inches from the roadway. They all were permitted by the State. Grady Green:

"If we were out there building that today, we wouldn't be allowed no poles that close to the curb."

On the subject of today, the JEA says it prefers underground installations in new areas, but on existing streets, JEA manager Dick Basford says, the concrete post with a 40-year life is the best buy:

"If you think about converting overhead to underground in an established area, the cost is tremendous. It's almost prohibitive to even think about it." Donaldson:

"Basically, a lot of public authorities, particularly utility companies, simply don't want to shoulder the cost of even making their things safe. They want to have them of a formidable size and strength so that if they are struck by a motorist, they are left in an unimpaired condition so it doesn't cost them a dime to do anything to repair them."

There is an alternative to the unyielding utility pole. A new model just undergone two years of testing at Texas A&M University. It's a breakaway version which researchers say will protect both motorists and utility lines. Two states, Texas and Massachusetts, are ready to try it out. In a head-on collision, the pole flips into the air, the car passes underneath, and the pole drops straight down. The section that's on hinges becomes a new base, leaving power and phone lines unbroken.

University engineer Don Ivey helped develop the pole:

"If the car drives under and you probably reduce the speed of the car less than 10 miles an hour, most of our tests—the speed changes about six miles an hour, which is no problem—would probably not cause any severe injury. Occasionally you might get a twisted wrist or something if you're holding onto the steering wheel a little tight."

Have you ever done any research or explored the idea of breakaway poles?

"No, we haven't. As a matter of fact, we go more the other way so they don't break away."

Basford points to power pole accidents like the one in St. Augustine in March where live wires were spilled onto the street, creating another hazard. And he said, we must remember, "poles don't hit cars. Cars hit poles."

The utility company tells you there's nothing that can be done, and people will just have to keep on hitting them. Well, obviously they don't care much about public safety."

"If people are observing the rules of the road . . . they're not drinking. They're driving within the speed limit and within weather conditions, visibility and rain. Ordinarily, they stay on the road. They got to get off the road in order to hit the pole. But any death is a tragedy and we are concerned about that, just as anyone else."

The feelings of the Greenwoods and the Micklers and thousands of other families who have lost loved ones in accidents go beyond concern.

"If there hadn't of been a pole here, quite likely our boys would be here today."

A footnote: Almost two weeks after we told the highway department about this fallen sign at I-95 and Hecksher, it's still here threatening passing traffic. Highways do not have to be this way. Shawn Briggs reports if you'll just drive north on our interstate you'll see a good example of that:

If the question is, can they build safer highways, the answer is, between Washington and Baltimore. I-95. Maryland state police report the main 30 mile stretch of interstate is remarkably safe.

Lieutenant Tom Wright:

"We haven't had any fatals at all this year, so far."

Consumer activists and federal officials agree. It is one of the best designed highways on the East Coast. Much of what highway engineers know about safety is built-in:

"Build a forgiving highway."

Clarke Bennett heads the Highway Safety Office of the Department of Transportation in Washington:

"As long as you got human beings out there driving cars, they're gonna err and so the idea is let's not make the error capital punishment."

More than half of all fatal accidents involve one car hitting something on the side of the road. F. J. Taminini is a highway engineer:

"About 85 percent of the vehicles hit something within say 30 feet of the highway. So if you can clear the highway 30 feet . . ."

It's called the clear roadsides concept. It is, simply, room to come to a stop before something stops you. This is what happens in a test car hitting a bridge abuttment. Bridge supports are the sixth worst man-made killer on roads today. On I-95 they're built back off the roadway. On older bridges there's a guard rail. In fact, rails are installed in front of any roadside danger that can't be moved out of the way. Unlike most guard rails on roads around Jacksonville, rails on I-95 have buried ends. Exposed ends become spears, literally, to a car going off the road. Still, the number-one man-made road side killer must be there.

"When you hit a light pole, it didn't give."

There are 130 million utility poles along U.S. roads. But, the driver who hit this one on I-95 was not hurt. It is a specially designed breakaway pole. When hit, the aluminum base gives. The pole flips up and away.

Nearly 300 of these breakaway poles were knocked down on this stretch of I-95 last year. Maryland officials know that because they had to put them back up again. But they don't have a great deal of first-hand testimony as to how well they work. State police say in 90 percent of the cases, the cars are so undamaged, the drivers unscratched, they simply knock the pole down and drive on their way.

Many or all of the safety concepts proven on I-95 can be applied to roads and highways around Jacksonville. Because the federal government has nearly completed its highway system, it's now pouring $13 billion a year into the states for improving local roads.

Roy Anderson, a former federal crash investigator, says local governments want the money but not safety advice.

"They don't like federal intervention. They think they're doing just fine the way they're doing. They think that safety is taken care of, and they want to get on with filling the potholes and paving the roads."

In the meantime, highway engineer Florrie Taminini uses his retirement to lobby for safety improvements with any group of highway professionals who will listen:

"For every dollar invested in safety improvement, they are getting that back in savings with regard to someone not being killed or injured or someone having a wage earner in a family continuing to work."

At Johns Hopkins University in Baltimore, injury prevention expert Susan Baker says through insurance rates and tax rates society pays $35 billion a year to the victims of highway accidents.

She thinks taxpayers should be demanding highway safety improvements:

"Saying to our county and state governments, we want better roads. Who's paying for them? Who's getting killed on them? It's the neighbors. It's the people who live in your county. I think it is absolutely reprehensible that we should simply make roads wider and smoother and capable of carrying more cars at faster speeds unless we, at the same time, are making those roads safer. Otherwise, we are just inviting the statistics to get worse. Otherwise, we are basically killing our grandchildren."

Commercial.

There are two ingredients that make up a dangerous road—the hazards along the side that we have already seen and the design of the road itself. When safety expert Gerry Donaldson was here, he looked at that aspect with Rob Sweeting:

"Anyone who accepts the roads in Jacksonville that I've seen the way that they are right now is simply rolling the dice every time he drives these roads."

That's how safety expert Gerry Donaldson feels about Jacksonville's roads after spending two days riding around. There are no hard and fast statistics that will tell you how many accidents occurred in Jacksonville or how many lives were lost solely because of poorly designed roads . . . but, experts like state design engineer Huey Hawkins will tell you, a bad road design can contribute to accidents:

"Back in those days when it was originally constructed, you know, it's the rate of acceleration . . ."

And city traffic engineer Henry Mock agrees:

"If the roadway, if the horizontal curvature or the vertical curvature of the roadway, is designed poorly, there's a number of things of this nature that could contribute to the accident."

Human error plays a big part in most accidents, but combined with a faulty or outdated road design, it could be deadly.

Perhaps the most glaring example of what can happen when

human error teams up with bad design was exemplified in this accident on the Buckman Bridge last summer. A truck driver and a passenger on a motorcycle were killed. The driver of the semi was traveling fast and tried to change lanes to avoid hitting a slow moving vehicle.

He struck a car and then a motorcycle. But after he made the mistake, there was nowhere for him to go because unlike some of the better designed bridges, the Buckman has virtually no recovery or emergency lanes. And a 6-inch curb, which was originally designed to stop motorists from going over the side, can actually serve as a launching pad.

"At the time it was constructed it was a good design. But according to today's standards, it obviously is a substandard design."

Eric Hooper's wife and two children were in an accident on the Buckman Bridge just last week.

They sat in slow-moving traffic and watched as a truck came barreling down the bridge. They were trapped, nowhere to go, unable to get out of the driver's way. His son was in a coma for more than 15 hours.

"He was pinned . . . his legs were pinned underneath him and he was just over in the seat unconscious. And because there was no access lane there they took him 30 minutes to get rescue and help out there to him and . . . it would be a bad situation for somebody to be that close to being . . . to dying and not have any help."

Just as poorly designed roads can lead to a high number of accidents, so can inadequate road signs. In fact, the Institute for Safety and Transportation out of New York estimates that a lack of road signs, confusing and misplaced signs, contribute to some 20,000 traffic deaths each year.

To demonstrate how poor signing, or in some cases no signs, can lead to driver confusion, we videotaped northbound traffic on I-95 near the Prudential Drive exit. Within minutes, there were several near misses . . . near misses that could have lead to accidents with injuries or deaths.

We showed the tape to Gerry Donaldson:

"Here, he is not given enough advance warning and the curb is not giving him enough horizontal safe distance, so that he can see the advanced poor design. It's a disaster."

But there is hope on the horizon. Plans are in the works to reconstruct this part of I-95 from the Fuller Warren toll bridge east just before Emerson Street. There is little hope, however, for the Arlington Expressway. Last year it had the third highest number of accidents, 46, of the city's most accident prone intersections and roads. It's a highway that even engineers who designed it will admit is hazardous.

"You have a number of off ramps coming off the Arlington Expressway onto and parallel to service roads. Those things are putting people in conflict with one another. To today's standard, we would change these things."

But if city and state highway engineers are aware of some of our dangerous roadways, why aren't we doing more to fix them?

"We have some roadway problems. We are trying to correct them as fast as money is made available. Until that money is available, then we're going to have to live with it."

But that's an argument some safety experts don't buy.

"When you have, as we know, a very high percentage of our accidents being caused not by vehicle to vehicle accidents, but by single vehicle run off the road encroachments, there is no excuse to allow those kinds of defects to persist in a chronic condition year after year."

CHAPTER 3

☙☙☙☙☙☙☙☙☙☙☙☙☙☙☙☙☙☙☙☙☙☙☙☙

Is It True?

Truth is a vaunted concept in journalism, but the definition of truth is not always as clear-cut as one might expect. For example:

- A press release from a candidate for the school board alleges that the current state of education in the city is very poor, as evidenced by the fact that half the students have below-average scores on a test of their reading levels. Is his statement true?

- A reporter doing a piece on a major battle interviews a corporal who details the heroism of his unit. Is the corporal's account true?

- A source who knows a nominee for the U.S. Supreme Court claims that the prospective judge has received a large sum of money from a financier who is in trouble with the law. But the source refuses to let you use his name. How do you know if the information is true?

It's apparent that there are many shades of truth, and—perhaps more important to a journalist—many shades of *provable* truth.[1]

The Concept of Truth

At the very heart of the examination of truth is the fact that a story can be constructed from correct information but convey a totally incorrect impression. The school board candidate, for example, may use valid facts to support a dubious conclusion.

---

1. See White et al. (1984), p. 55, for further discussion of provable truth.

The candidate's contention that half the scores of district students are below average leaves a strong impression that education is substandard. But a reporter looking for a critical standard of truth would recognize that often *in popular usage* "average" is meant to refer to a point where half are above and half are below. (See the discussion of "averages" in chapter 5.)

Lines of truth and falsity are equally blurred when the reporter considers the veracity of a statement by a witness. The example of the corporal in battle is a well-known dilemma faced by historians as well as journalists.[2] Historians know full well that the limited perspective of a participant in a battle may lead that soldier into drawing some unwarranted conclusions; taking the foot-soldier's word as fact can lead the historian or reporter astray. Even if the soldier is willing to tell the truth, his personal perspective may strongly color his perception of the truth.

Applications: How Experienced Journalists Sort Out the Truth

A problem closely related to the corporal-on-the-battlefield example was faced by Richard Petrow, executive producer of the recent PBS "In Search of the Constitution with Bill Moyers" series and professor of journalism at New York University. Petrow wrote a book about the Nazi occupation of Norway and Denmark during World War II titled *The Bitter Years.* During several years of research, he conducted interviews with hundreds of people who recounted their experiences during the war years—people who sometimes gave conflicting views as to what had actually happened. Petrow developed a particular standard of judgment for evaluating the truth of what he heard: the level of the interviewee's self-interest.

"If, when they talked about the war years, they revealed themselves as timid, cowardly, or reluctant to get involved, I tended to believe them," Petrow said. "But if they portrayed

---

2. See Marc Bloch (1964), pp. 48–60, for a discussion of how historians evaluate reliability of this type of incident.

3.1 Richard Petrow, Professor, Department of Journalism,
New York University.

themselves as heroes, I tended to disbelieve them unless confirmed by other evidence."[3]

Petrow's instincts about people and their motives also played
a role in his evaluation of a story that came to him when he
worked as a television journalist. A source informed him that
a local politician was about to be indicted on criminal charges.
Petrow could obtain no official confirmation but decided he
would run the story primarily because "the source did not have
an ax to grind." In other words, the source of the information

---

3. Recounted by Petrow (1987).

did not stand to gain by the politician's embarrassment. In addition, Petrow noted that the source had access to the indictment process and had been truthful in the past. Also, the story itself was believable because the politician had been involved in previous dealings "on the outskirts of legality." (As an interesting sidelight, Petrow could not get the story cleared for air by the station's legal counsel. "Cautious lawyers," he explained. But because he felt it served the public interest, he gave the story to a friend who worked on *The New York Post*. The paper printed the story. Petrow then used the newspaper story as a means of persuading the station's lawyers to permit him to cover the story with additional follow-up material. Eventually, the source's information proved to be true. The politician was indicted.)

It becomes apparent that the believability of a witness hinges to a great extent on his or her vested interests, or, as historian Marc Bloch describes it, "the willingness to tell the truth."[4] Someone with a vested interest may be less than willing to tell the truth, as in the case of the candidate for a school board who wants to leave the impression that the incumbents are doing a poor job of promoting quality education, or the participant in the battle, who will probably have an interest in portraying his own heroism.

Historians such as Bloch also make a distinction regarding the witness's *ability* to tell the truth. Can a witness give an objective report of a traffic accident? Possibly, but as any reporter who has had to deal with second-hand accounts quickly comes to realize, the witness who has just seen his first traffic accident is likely to be overwhelmed by the noise, violence, and suffering and may unintentionally exaggerate the description of what could actually be a relatively minor mishap. It stands to reason, then, that historians and journalists would prefer the accident description provided by a traffic cop to that of an inexperienced bystander. The bystander's lack of perspective impairs his or her ability to tell the truth.

Along the same lines, it is vitally important for a journalist to distinguish between a *document* and an *instrument* when

---

4. From Bloch's (1964), pp. 48–78, discussion on the evaluation and transmission of evidence.

evaluating truthfulness.[5] A *document* is generally taken to be something which describes; it does not have a hidden agenda and does not exist for any other reason than to inform. A court transcript is an example of a document. An *instrument* has a purpose other than to describe or inform; it generally exists to elicit a certain type of reaction or further a particular goal. Most press releases are instruments.

To complete the discussion, consider again the problem of the anonymous source. Many sources refuse to disclose their names because of fear for their jobs or reputations. But as a result of their anonymity, they cannot be held direcly accountable for untruths they issue accidentally or on purpose. The journalist who reprints comments from an anonymous source, or uses them on the air, runs a risk of repeating information which may be totally untrue to untrue to a degree.

But some stories probably would not be possible without the anonymous source. The example of the Supreme Court nominee was one real case: In 1969, it was disclosed through an anonymous source that court nominee Abe Fortas had received $20,000 from a financier who was himself in trouble with the Securities and Exchange Commission. *Los Angeles Times* reporter Ronald Ostrow, speaking before an Associated Press managing editors panel, maintained that this and several other of his stories could never have been written without anonymous sources.[6]

All journalists do not agree with that contention, however. Some claim that almost any story can be written with information given from sources who allow their names to be used—even when dealing with highly controversial topics. For example, *The Pittsburgh Press* undertook a ten-month investigation of the buying and selling of human kidneys worldwide and decided from the start not to use any unattributed sources.[7] Series co-author Andrew Schneider told the *Washington Journalism Review* that

---

5. Standard knowledge, but explained to author in some detail by Schulte (1987).
6. Detailed by Stein (1987), Ostrow quoted p. 17.
7. Described by Leslie (1986).

the decision was based on a desire to produce entirely credible material. "It's really hard to talk about fictionalizing something or taking it out of context when you've got a couple of hundred doctors, nurses, procurement people, and donor families all talking [on the record] about the issues at hand" (Leslie, 1986, p. 33).

And although he supports some uses of anonymous sources, even Ronald Ostrow warns of the dangers. Because there is no real accountability if the source provides false or distorted information, Ostrow warns, "We are opening ourselves to being used by officials with an ax to grind or a turf war to wage" (Stein, 1987, p. 17).

Because of the danger of a source providing information which is false by intent or simply because sources may not understand the concept of full truth, most veterans will not use information from only one unnamed source unless there is documentary evidence to bolster the case.

It's apparent that the truth issue is nowhere near as clear-cut as it might seem on the surface. However, experienced journalists do have some general guidelines for determining the truth of information or conclusions.

Criteria: Is It True?

While this list is far from airtight, considering each of the questions may help you determine the veracity of information.

1. Is the source of the information capable of telling the truth? In other words, does he or she know enough about the situation to give you an accurate recounting of what happened? As mentioned above, the first-time witness to a car accident is unlikely to give as objective a view as a traffic cop, who is a veteran observer. If the story involves legalities, does the source understand those legalities? Does he or she realize, for example, that someone charged in a death is not necessarily charged with *murder?*

2. Is the source of the information willing to tell the truth? Does he or she have the proverbial "ax to grind"? Does the source, to the best of your knowledge, stand to benefit from disclosure of the information? If so, the information may be false

or seriously distorted; even basically honest people tend to repeat information in a light which shines favorably on themselves. Along the same lines, be wary of sources who refuse to let you use their names. In some cases, their reluctance stems from the fact that they are not willing to tell you the whole truth. Push for "on the record" comments whenever possible (quotes that will be directly attributed to the speaker).

3. If written or printed materials are offered, are they documents or instruments? Were they prepared solely for the purpose of recounting information, or was there some other reason for their existence?

4. Does the information come from a variety of sources? A journalist sees information in different ways than most people do. He or she often poses the same question to different people, even in social situations. (This constantly irritates spouses, who claim, "But John (or Susan) already told you that!" to which the journalist typically replies, "But I want to hear Susan's (John's) version.")

The point is that five members of a particular interest group may recount the same story in the same way, but their numbers should not tip your information-weighing scales nearly as much as the same information from five unrelated sources.

5. Can you confirm the information from an unsolicited source? The information provided from people who call a newsroom is quite different in character from what is provided by people who are called by a reporter. When in doubt about information someone offers you, one verification strategy is to call someone who should know but is unrelated to the original source of the information, and ask for confirmation.

6. Does the information or the source strike you as fishy? To use the fish analogy, the only reliable way for inspectors to tell if fish is spoiling is to have someone with an "accurate" nose smell it. Journalists quickly develop an accurate nose, too, meaning that if their instincts tell them there is something wrong with the information or the source, there probably is. Your people-reading skills are likely to be far more developed than you might imagine.

The tip-off may be seemingly insignificant. One reporter notes that he "started picking up a foul odor" because one person had exaggerated his height on his resume. Use your senses and your knowledge of people—stay alert.

Case History: Covering the Kennedy Assassination

The shots that rang out over Dealey Plaza in Dallas on November 22, 1963, changed history and, to an extent, changed the complexion of news itself. The assassination of President John F. Kennedy was a story that broke before the watching eyes of the public. In a sense, those of us who watched the horror story unfold were all participants in the tragedy, close observers of the news-gathering process.

The New York Times is regarded as a newspaper of record; that is, a record of the world's history written day-by-day, and that stature places an enormous responsibility on reporters and editors. Here's how Tom Wicker, a reporter (later columnist) with the *Times*, gathered his facts and compiled what may have been the biggest story of his life.

Wicker's recounting of the Kennedy assassination is a classic example of how experienced reporters gather information and decide on its veracity. While reading Wicker's account, note these points:

1. Although Wicker was in the motorcade press bus, he was not an eyewitness to most of the events of the day. He gathered his information from speaking to others, exchanging details with other reporters, even by listening to the radio.

2. Wicker had no magic sieve with which to separate fact from fiction. He could do only what any of us would do: listen, match what we've heard to see if it squares with other information, and use our best judgment as to the reliability of the source.

3. Wicker had to deal with some false information. Note how the original statement from the doctors who treated President Kennedy proved to be erroneous.

4. The composition of the story was a work in progress. Although he was essentially meeting one deadline, Wicker wrote, rewrote, and filled in holes on his original story while he gathered and verified facts.

I think I was in the first press bus. But I can't be sure. Pete Lisagor of the *Chicago Daily News* says he *knows* he was in the first press

---

3.2   Tom Wicker, *New York Times.*

bus and he describes things that went on aboard it that didn't happen on the bus I was in. But I still *think* I was in the first press bus.

I cite that minor confusion as an example of the way it was in Dallas in the early afternoon of November 22. At first no one knew what happened, or how, or where, much less why. Gradually, bits and pieces began to fall together and within two hours a reasonably coherent version of the story began to be possible. Even now, however, I know no reporter who was there who has a clear and orderly picture of that surrealistic afternoon; it is still a matter of bits and pieces thrown hastily into something like a whole.

It began, for most reporters, when the central fact of it was over. As our press bus eased at motorcade speed down an incline toward an underpass, there was a little confusion in the sparse crowds that at that point had been standing at the curb to see the President of the United States pass. As we came out of the underpass, I saw a motorcycle policeman drive over the curb, across an open area, a few feet up a railroad bank, dismount, and start scrambling up the bank.

Jim Mathis of The Advance (Newhouse) Syndicate went to the front of our bus and looked ahead to where the President's car was supposed to be, perhaps ten cars ahead of us. He hurried back to his seat.

"The President's car just sped off," he said. "Really gunned away." (How could Mathis have seen that if there had been another bus in front of us?)

But that could have happened if someone had thrown a tomato at the President. The press bus in its stately pace rolled on to the Trade Mart, where the President was to speak. Fortunately, it was only a few minutes away.

At the Trade Mart, rumor was sweeping the hundreds of Texans already eating their lunch. It was the only rumor that I had ever *seen;* it was moving across that crowd like a wind over a wheat-field. A man eating a grapefruit seized my arm as I passed.

"Has the President been shot?" he asked.

"I don't think so," I said. "But something happened."

With the other reporters—I suppose thirty-five of them—I went on through the huge hall to the upstairs press room. We were hardly there when Marianne Means of Hearst Headline Service hung up a telephone, ran to a group of us and said, "The President's been shot. He's at Parkland Hospital."

One thing I learned that day; I suppose I already knew it, but that day made it plain. A reporter must trust his instinct. When Miss Means said those eight words—I never learned who told her*—I knew absolutely they were true. Everyone did. We ran for the press buses.

Again, a man seized my arm—an official-looking man.

---

*After this was published, Marianne Means told me she had called her office in New York and had heard the news from there. The New York office had heard a radio bulletin. By that roundabout route, the motorcade press learned what had happened.

Is It True?

"No running in here," he said sternly. I pulled free and ran on. Doug Kiker of the *Herald Tribune* barreled head-on into a waiter carrying a plate of potatoes. Waiter and potatoes flew about the room. Kiker ran on. He was in his first week with the *Trib*, and his first presidential trip.

I barely got aboard a moving press bus. Bob Pierrepoint of CBS was aboard and he said that he now recalled having heard something that could have been shots—or firecrackers, or motorcycle backfire. We talked anxiously, unbelieving, afraid.

Fortunately again, it was only a few minutes to Parkland Hospital. There at its emergency entrance, stood the President's car, the top up, a bucket of bloody water beside it. Automatically, I took down its license number—GG300 District of Columbia.

The first eyewitness description came from Senator Ralph Yarborough, who had been riding in the third car of the motorcade with Vice-President and Mrs. Johnson. Senator Yarborough is an East Texan, which is to say a Southerner, a man of quick emotion, old-fashioned rhetoric.

"Gentlemen," he said, pale, shaken, near tears. "It's a deed of horror."

The details he gave us were good and mostly—as it later proved—accurate. But he would not describe to us the appearance of the President as he was wheeled into the hospital, except to say that he was "gravely wounded." We could not doubt, then, that it was serious.

I had chosen that day to be without a notebook. I took notes on the back of my mimeographed schedule of the two-day tour of Texas we had been so near to concluding. Today, I cannot read many of the notes; on November 22, they were as clear as 60-point type.

A local television reporter, Mel Crouch, told us he had seen a rifle being withdrawn from the corner fifth- or sixth-floor window of the Texas School Book Depository. Instinct again—Crouch sounded right, positive, though none of us knew him. We believed it and it was right.

Mac Kilduff, an assistant White House press secretary in charge of the press on that trip, and who was to acquit himself well that day, came out of the hospital. We gathered round and he told us the President was alive. It wasn't true, we later learned; but Mac thought it was true at that time, and he didn't mislead us about a possible recovery. His whole demeanor made plain what was likely to happen. He also told us—as Senator Yarborough had—that Governor John Connally of Texas was shot, too.

Kilduff promised more details in five minutes and went back into the hospital. We were barred. Word came to us secondhand—I don't remember exactly how—from Bob Clark of ABC, one of the men who had been riding in the press "pool" car near the President's, that he had been lying face-down in Mrs. Kennedy's lap when the car arrived at Parkland. No signs of life.

That is what I mean by instinct. That day, a reporter had none of the ordinary means or time to check and double-check matters given as fact. He had to go on what he knew of people he talked to, what he knew of human reaction, what two isolated "facts" added to in sum—above all on what he felt in his bones. I knew Clark and respected him. I took his report at face value, even at second hand. It turned out to be true. In a crisis, if a reporter can't trust his instinct for truth, he can't trust anything.

When Wayne Hawks of the White House staff appeared to say that a press room had been set up in a hospital classroom at the left rear of the building, the group of reporters began struggling across the lawn in that direction. I lingered to ask a motorcycle policeman if he had heard on his radio anything about the pursuit or capture of the assassin. He hadn't, and I followed the other reporters.

As I was passing the open convertible in which Vice-President and Mrs. Johnson and Senator Yarborough had been riding in the motorcade, a voice boomed from its radio:

"The President of the United States is dead. I repeat—it has just been announced that the President of the United States is dead."

There was no authority, no word of who had announced it. But—instinct again—I believed it instantly. It sounded true. I knew it was true. I stood still a moment, then began running.

Ordinarily, I couldn't jump a tennis net if I'd just beaten Gonzales. That day, carrying a briefcase and a typewriter, I jumped a chain fence looping around the drive, not even breaking stride. Hugh Sidey of *Time*, a close friend of the President, was walking slowly ahead of me.

"Hugh," I said, "the President's dead. Just announced on the radio. I don't know who announced it but it sounded official to me."

Sidey stopped, looked at me, looked at the ground. I couldn't talk about it. I couldn't think about it. I couldn't do anything but run on to the press room. Then I told others what I had heard.

Is It True?

Sidey, I learned a few minutes later, stood where he was a minute. Then he saw two Catholic priests. He spoke to them. Yes, they told him, the President was dead. They had administered the last rites. Sidey went on to the press room and spread that word, too.

Throughout the day, every reporter on the scene seemed to me to do his best to help everyone else. Information came only in bits and pieces. Each man who picked up a bit or a piece passed it on. I know no one who held anything out. Nobody thought about an exclusive; it didn't seem important.

After perhaps ten minutes when we milled around in the press room—my instinct was to find the new President, but no one knew where he was—Kilduff appeared red-eyed, barely in control of himself. In that hushed classroom, he made the official, the unbelievable announcement. The President was dead of a gunshot wound in the brain. Lyndon Johnson was safe, in protective custody of the Secret Service. He would be sworn in as soon as possible.

Kilduff, composed as a man could be in those circumstances, promised more details when he could get them, then left. The search for phones began. Jack Gertz, traveling with us for AT&T, was frantically moving them by the dozen into the hospital, but few were ready yet.

I wandered down the hall, found a doctor's office, walked in and told him I had to use his phone. He got up without a word and left. I battled the hospital switchboard for five minutes and finally got a line to New York—Hal Faber on the other end, with Harrison Salisbury on an extension.

They knew what had happened, I said. The death had been confirmed. I proposed to write one long story, as quickly as I could, throwing in everything I could learn. On the desk, they could cut it up as they needed—throwing part into other stories, putting other facts into mine. But I would file a straight narrative without worrying about their editing needs.

Reporters always fuss at editors and always will. But Salisbury and Faber are good men to talk to in a crisis. They knew what they were doing and realized my problems. I may fuss at them again sometime, but after that day my heart won't be in it. Quickly, clearly, they told me to go ahead, gave me the moved-up deadlines, told me of plans already made to get other reporters into Dallas, but made it plain they would be hours in arriving.

Salisbury told me to use the phone and take no chances on a wire circuit being jammed or going wrong. Stop reporting and start writing in time to meet the deadline, he said. Pay anyone $50 if necessary to dictate for you.

The whole conversation probably took three minutes. Then I hung up, thinking of all there was to know, all there was I didn't know. I wandered down a corridor and ran into Sidey and Chuck Roberts of *Newsweek*. They'd seen a hearse pulling up at the emergency entrance and we figured they were about to move the body.

We made our way to the hearse—a Secret Service agent who knew us helped us through suspicious Dallas police lines—and the driver said his instructions were to take the body to the airport. That confirmed our hunch, but gave me, at least, another wrong one. Mr. Johnson, I declared, would fly to Washington with the body and be sworn in there.

We posted ourselves inconspicuously near the emergency entrance. Within minutes, they brought the body out in a bronze coffin.

A number of White House staff people—stunned, silent, stumbling along as if dazed—walked with it. Mrs. Kennedy walked by the coffin, her hand on it, her head down, her hat gone, her dress and stockings spattered. She got into the hearse with the coffin. The staff men crowded into cars and followed.

That was just about the only eyewitness matter that I got with my own eyes that entire afternoon.

Roberts commandeered a seat in a police car and followed, promising to "fill" Sidey and me as necessary. We made the same promise to him and went back to the press room.

There, we received an account from Julian Reed, a staff assistant, of Mrs. John Connally's recollection of the shooting. Most of his recital was helpful and it established the important fact of who was sitting in which seat in the President's car at the time of the shooting.

The doctors who had treated the President came in after Mr. Reed. They gave us copious detail, particularly as to the efforts they had made to resuscitate the President. They were less explicit about the wounds, explaining that the body had been in their hands only a short time and they had little time to examine it closely. They conceded they were unsure as to the time of death and had arbitrarily put it at 1:00 p.m., CST.

Much of their information, as it developed later, was erroneous.

Is It True?

Subsequent reports made it pretty clear that Mr. Kennedy probably was killed instantly. His body, as a physical mechanism, however, continued to flicker an occasional pulse and heartbeat. No doubt this justified the doctors' first account. There also was the question of national security and Mr. Johnson's swearing-in. Perhaps, too, there was a question about the Roman Catholic rites. In any case, until a later doctors' statement about 9:00 p.m. that night, the account we got at the hospital was official.

The doctors hardly had left before Hawks came in and told us Mr. Johnson would be sworn in immediately at the airport. We dashed for the press buses, still parked outside. Many a campaign had taught me something about press buses and I ran a little harder, got there first, and went to the wide rear seat. That is the best place on a bus to open up a typewriter and get some work done.

On the short trip to the airport, I got about five hundred words on paper—leaving a blank space for the hour of Mr. Johnson's swearing-in, and putting down the mistaken assumption that the scene would be somewhere in the terminal. As we arrived at the back gate along the airstrip, we could see *Air Force One*, the presidential jet, screaming down the runway and into the air.

Left behind had been Sid Davis of Westinghouse Broadcasting, one of the few reporters who had been present for the swearing-in. Roberts, who had guessed right in going to the airport when he did, had been there too and was aboard the plane on the way to Washington.

Davis climbed on the back of a shiny new car that was parked near where our bus halted. I hate to think what happened to its trunk deck. He and Roberts—true to his promise—had put together a magnificent "pool" report on the swearing-in. Davis read it off, answered questions, and gave a picture that so far as I know was complete, accurate and has not yet been added to.

I said to Kiker of the *Trib:* "We better go write. There'll be phones in the terminal." He agreed. Bob Manning, an ice-cool member of the White House transportation staff, agreed to get our bags off the press plane, which would return to Washington as soon as possible, and put them in a nearby telephone booth.

Kiker and I ran a half-mile to the terminal, cutting through a baggage-handling room to get there. I went immediately to a phone booth and dictated my five-hundred-word lead, correcting it as I read, embellishing it too. Before I hung up, I got Salisbury and asked him to cut into my story whatever the wires were filing on the assassin. There was not time left to chase down the Dallas police and find out those details on my own.

Dallas's Love Field has a mezzanine running around its main waiting room; it is equipped with writing desks for travelers. I took one and went to work. My recollection is that it was then about 5:00 p.m. New York time.

I would write two pages, run down the stairs, across the waiting room, grab a phone and dictate. Miraculously, I never had to wait for a phone booth or to get a line through. Dictating each take, I would throw in items I hadn't written, sometimes whole paragraphs. It must have been tough on the dictating room crew.

Once, while in the booth dictating, I looked up and found twitching above me the imposing mustache of Gladwin Hill. He was the first *Times* man in and had found me right off; I was seldom more glad to see anyone. We conferred quickly and he took off for the police station; it was a tremendous load off my mind to have that angle covered and out of my hands.

I was half through, maybe more, when I heard myself paged. It turned out to be Kiker, who had been separated from me and was working in the El Dorado Room, a bottle club in the terminal. My mezzanine was quieter and a better place to work, but he had a TV going for him, so I moved in too.

The TV helped in one important respect. I took down from it an eyewitness account of one Charles Drehm, who had been waving at the President when he was shot. Instinct again: Drehm sounded positive, right, sure of what he said. And his report was the first real indication that the President probably was shot twice.

Shortly after 7:00 p.m., New York time, I finished. So did Kiker. Simultaneously we thought of our bags out in that remote phone booth. We ran for a taxi and urged an unwilling driver out along the dark airstrip. As we found the place, with some difficulty, an American Airlines man was walking off with the bags. He was going to ship them off to the White House, having seen the tags on them. A minute later and we'd have been stuck in Dallas without even a toothbrush.

Kiker and I went to the *Dallas News*. The work wasn't done—I filed a number of inserts later that night, wrote a separate story on the building from which the assassin had fired, tried to get John Herbers, Don Janson, Joe Loftus on useful angles as they drifted in. But when I left the airport, I knew the worst of it was over. The story was filed on time, good or bad, complete or incomplete, and any reporter knows how that feels. They couldn't say I missed the deadline.

It was a long taxi ride to the *Dallas News.* We were hungry, not having eaten since an early breakfast. It was then that I remembered John F. Kennedy's obituary. Last June, Hal Faber had sent it to me for updating. On November 22, it was still lying on my desk in Washington, not updated, not rewritten, a monument to the incredibility of that afternoon in Dallas.

CHAPTER 4

◌◌◌◌◌◌◌◌◌◌◌◌◌◌◌◌◌◌◌◌◌◌◌◌◌◌

Is It Fair?

- Governor Smith charges that Mayor Jones has totally mishandled several hundred thousand dollars' worth of state funding. You use that quote in a newscast; in fact, it makes up your whole story about the funds situation. Did you handle it fairly?

- You cover a city council meeting where the agenda calls for discussion of the preparations for the upcoming primary election. A shouting match breaks out between the city manager and the city clerk about whose department will pay for certain aspects of the election. You give extensive coverage to the shouting match but do not focus on the election issue per se. Is this a fair and complete way to present the issue?

- During coverage of a civil disturbance, you tour the affected areas of the city in a police car. You are generally given VIP treatment. Can you produce a fair, objective story relying solely on what you learn from this observation?

Fairness is not a particularly easy concept to define; in fact, it is all too easy to scream "unfair!" when a news story differs with someone's point of view, or in the popular parlance, gores someone's ox. But several principles of fairness do emerge, and learning how seasoned journalists gauge the fairness of their work can help you develop the right instincts.

What Is Fairness?

Good question, and a tough one. Under the heading "fair play" in the code of ethics of the Society of Professional Journalists, we are advised that: "Journalists at all times will show respect for the dignity, privacy, rights, and well-being of people encountered in the course of gathering and presenting the news." Also in that section, the Society of Professional Journalists advocates that the news media shall not communicate unofficial charges "affecting reputation or moral character without giving the accused a chance to reply."

Any working journalist knows that these canons were not concocted in a vacuum. To an extent, they reflect a preplanned response to everyday situations. For example, consider the patent unfairness of running the charge of the governor without offering the mayor a chance to reply. High office does not give the holder privilege to make personal attacks and to have those attacks go unchallenged. Indeed, this is a relatively easy puzzle: Of course the mayor has a right to reply. In fact, some newspapers, under news department policy, would not print the governor's comments until the mayor had been contacted for a reply.

But let's dissect a more difficult application of fairness, an issue addressed in Article Two of the Code of Ethics of the Radio-Television News Directors Association:

> Broadcast news presentations shall be designed not only to offer timely and accurate information, but also to present it in light of relevant circumstances that give it meaning and perspective.

If you zeroed in on the shouting match at the city council meeting, you may have missed the real story—a story which could have involved hundreds of thousands of dollars of taxpayer money spent on a municipal primary election. How was that money allocated? Were election plans properly designed and implemented? Is there really a need for the expense of a primary election that would only eliminate four candidates? Those are the real questions. The personality clash of the city officials, while possibly symptomatic of a deeper problem, is peripheral.

Problems related to putting events in their proper context commonly surface between journalists and government officials, and perhaps more commonly, between journalists and business people. Often the government or business official who complains that you didn't get the whole story means "you didn't tell it the way I wanted it," but he or she often expresses the valid complaint that the essential core of the story was missed by a journalist who focused on a detail. Journalists *do* miss stories because they don't understand or bother to report the larger set of circumstances that puts events in perspective.

Note how different a journalist's point of view can be, depending upon where he or she sits. A reporter who views a disturbance entirely from the back seat of a patrol car, for example, will usually get the police view of the event. The police officers, themselves, will most likely be hand-picked by a media-savvy public relations officer. What you see and hear will probably be carefully planned in advance.

Applying Standards of Fairness, Completeness, and Objectivity

One of the best examples of how perspectives are altered is provided by Theodore H. White (1978), a venerable foreign correspondent, who recalled his closeup coverage of warfare in China in 1939[1]:

> The Ministry of Information was happy to give me leave. I think my prying had begun to annoy them. They issued me a low-grade military pass to visit the war areas and arranged an airplane ticket to take me to Sian, where I would be on my own to make my way to the war front two hundred and fifty miles beyond. I was lucky the pass was of such low quality. Had I been granted the VIP pass usually given to famous correspondents and dignitaries, I would have been escorted to the war front and back in style and seen

1. White (1978) offers an interesting perspective on objectivity on pp. 84–101.

nothing—as happened to me in the Vietnam War, thirty years later, after I had become known and cocooned from reality. (p. 85)

Vietnam coverage would certainly involve correspondents being "cocooned"; reporters literally had to risk their lives and reputations to get news that the government wanted to keep from them. Harrison Salisbury of *The New York Times* was, in 1966, bitterly repudiated by some other members of the press for his trip to Hanoi and his resultant article about American bombing raids on Christmas Eve. But, as James Boylan (1986), former editor of the *Columbia Journalism Review*, pointed out, Salisbury had "served the purpose of enforcing candor by extending media coverage to include not only the bombardier but the bombed" (p. 35). Boylan notes that this was in "healthy contrast to what Michael H. Arlen of *The New Yorker* called the glamourization on the television networks of the air war . . ." (p. 5).

Problems with fairness, objectivity, and completeness are obviously not limited to the battlefield. Newspaper copy editors, for example, devote a major portion of their working day to looking for *holes* in stories—areas where the information is not complete or the impression is not fair. For example, a copy editor will instantly flag a charge made with no reply. Alert editors will spot more subtle unanswered questions. A line of copy such as:

State College President John J. Smith, who lives in a 15-room mansion overlooking City Park, feels that the park rezoning issue . . .

will elicit this question from the copy editor:

Hey, where does Smith get the money to afford a 15-room mansion in that neighborhood? State college presidents don't make that kind of money!

Which might bring about his addition to the copy:

Is It Fair?

State College President John J. Smith, a former senior partner of a major law firm who left corporate law to enter academics five years ago, lives in a 15-room mansion overlooking City Park. He feels that the park rezoning issue . . .[2]

The questioning mind of the copy editor prodded the reporter to produce a complete story, a story that is fair in that it does not raise suggestions of impropriety on the part of the college president. In other words, it does not leave the reader wondering if he is siphoning state funds to pay for his mansion. In fact, some copy editors will quibble with the word *mansion* itself. Could a better word be found, a word that does not carry the same loaded connotation?

These are the types of decisions a journalist has to make in evaluating a story's fairness, completeness, and objectivity. The following list of questions may serve as a starting point for you when evaluating your own work.

Criteria: Is It Fair?

1. Does the story present the overall perspective? Carefully evaluate whether the real issues or the "cosmetics," the peripheral features, have taken center stage. Don't lead with a story on a shouting match when what led to the confrontation is a much bigger story. Some similar aspects of this issue will be examined in the upcoming chapter on distortion.

2. Are there any questions left unanswered or major issues left uncovered? The story has never been written or taped which answers *all* the questions which might be raised, and in most cases the clock is the final arbiter of completeness. But in all cases, avoid charges levelled but never answered. (You do not need to seek responses to official legal charges, such as

---

2. Copy editing example loosely based on incident experienced by author when writing for *The Worcester Telegram*, 1985.

indictments or court verdicts.) Always be mindful of the seemingly small questions, such as the college president's mansion.

3. Is my perspective objective? Objectivity is a thorny issue, but it is safe to assume that if your observations have been controlled in some way, your view is not totally fair.

4. Is my intent objective? Be sure that your personal feelings do not cloud your treatment of the story. One reporter recalls with some regret his treatment in print of a singer who was, in the reporter's view, "the snottiest thing going." As a result, the reporter wrote what he today characterized as "a snotty story." If indeed the singer was as much of a heel as the story portrayed, there are other ways to get that story, including talking to others for their impressions. Beware the revenge motive.

5. Do I have enough material on which to base the story? A story based on one observation or one perspective (such as number 4 above) runs the risk of being unfair and incomplete. In addition to the fairness problem, there may be serious omissions of facts, and those can obviously erode the quality and value of a reporter's work. For example, a writer was working on a piece about health care plans.[3] Close to the time he was to finish the story, he found that on a local college campus there was an organization devoted solely to the study of local health insurance and health plans. He debated whether or not to call—after all, the story was almost finished and seemed complete—but decided to make contact. He found a completely new perspective on the story and discovered that the organization was a major mover in the local health care system. The story would have been ludicrously incomplete had not that contact been made. The writer, far from an expert on health plans, did not realize this until after he had made himself an expert on the whole issue. So ask more questions than you think you need to. Gather as many clippings as you can carry. Talk to as many people and as wide a variety of people as possible when compiling a story.

---

3. From author's experience as a writer for *Worcester Magazine*, 1987.

Case History: The Wee Care Day Nursery Trial

As noted in this chapter (particularly, checklist points 2 and 5), deciding how much information is enough is a particularly difficult call for an editor or reporter.

Diane Curcio, the court and county government reporter for the Newark, New Jersey, *Star-Ledger*, was confronted with exactly that problem during her coverage of a case which involved the alleged sexual abuse of children in a Maplewood, New Jersey, day care center.

The crux of the dilemma was the graphic nature of the testimony. Curcio noted that editors would sometimes eliminate graphic detail or describe the alleged abuse in generic terms. As a result, Curcio felt that the omission of information tended to slant certain aspects of the story. "I had defense attorneys who had read accounts of the trial tell me 'that's not much of a case.' I got the feeling that readers did not get the full impact of the testimony."

She also noted that toning down the descriptions of abuse cut both ways. "The defense's contention was that the acts alleged to have occurred at the nursery school were just too bizarre—they couldn't have happened given the time and space limitations at the school. So, by not fully reporting the testimony, I could be doing a disservice to the defense as well as to the prosecution."

Either way, she felt that the reading public would be best served by the most complete description of the testimony. She acknowledged that deciding the level of graphic sexual detail to run in a general-readership paper is not an easy call, and felt that the *Star-Ledger* was courageous in committing a reporter to cover such a highly sensitive story on a daily basis. She also pointed out that the amount of editing done to the story often depended on the editorial personnel on duty the particular nights her stories were filed; as a result, the level of graphic description tended to vary from day to day.

What's your opinion? Compare "Detective quizzed in day-care sex abuse trial," in which descriptions of sexual acts were edited and abuse described in generic terms (which, Curcio felt, left the reader puzzled as to exactly what was supposed to have happened), to "Mom tells nursery sex trial her son played nude 'game' at pal's party," in which quite graphic descriptions were used.

Mom tells nursery sex trial her son played nude 'game' at pal's party

By Diane Curcio

A mother testified in Superior Court in Newark yesterday that before allegations were raised of sexual abuse at Wee Care Day Nursery in Maplewood she saw her son take off his pants and play a "pile-up game" at a friend's birthday party.

Former students from the defunct Maplewood nursery have testified their teacher Margaret Kelly Michaels engaged them in the nude game during which children would lay on top of one another. Using dolls in the judge's chambers, the children, who were ages three and four when the offenses allegedly happened, sometimes showed how "pile-up" was played.

The mother testifying yesterday in Newark said that at the birthday party her son "had his pants down and a little blonde child with a chunky rear end and he was laying on top of her." She said other mothers saw it too and "I was so embarrassed. . . All the kids were around there playing like nothing happened, like it was normal behavior."

This birthday party happened on May 4, 1985, according to a stipulation read to the jury. That was three days before another Wee Care preschooler had a routine doctor's visit and mentioned to a nurse taking his temperature rectally that his teacher did the same thing. His remarks touched off the investigation that resulted in three indictments being handed up against the 24-year-old Michaels, accusing her of sexually assaulting and threatening 20 children. The children said they were molested with knives, forks and spoons during naptime and in bathrooms.

The mother yesterday said she knew nothing of the other boy's remark when the incident happened at the birthday party.

Her six-year-old son also testified yesterday, via closed circuit television in Superior Court. The boy said he would draw a picture to tell Judge William F. Harth something about his former teacher. But when Essex County Assistant Prosecutor Glenn D. Goldberg asked the child to identify what part of the female anatomy he had drawn under the stick figure's neck, the boy balked.

First, he said he didn't know what it was, then he said it was a "toy." Ultimately, the child whispered into Harth's ear that he had drawn "breasts." The boy had said it was a picture of Michaels.

Twice during his testimony the boy said he was "getting sleepy." He said boys and girls played the "pile-up game." When asked if anyone ever touched him at Wee Care, the boy got up in his chair and pointed to his genitals.

"They touched people in their private parts," he said. Goldberg asked: "Who did that?" and the boy said, "Kelly."

The child is named as a victim in eight counts of the indictment, alleging assorted acts of sexual assault. Defense attorney Harvey Meltzer cross-examined him about each alleged incident and the boy denied they occurred.

When the mother took the stand, however, she said her son had disclosed the incidents to her. The boy told social workers and investigators initially that he had not been abused. During the summer of 1985 he slowly revealed his involvement to his mother, she said. He brought up the subject while they were watching a children's program on television one Saturday morning, the mother testified.

Throughout the 1984-85 school year, the mother said she noticed behavioral changes in her son, who was classified as a gifted child before his enrollment in Wee Care. The mother said she and her husband made "sacrifices" to pay the $175 monthly tuition for her son because they hoped his three days a week at the school would nurture his talents. The parents were in family counseling to resolve their differences when the boy was enrolled in the Maplewood nursery.

While at Wee Care, she said he became a "clean freak," who wanted to change his clothes often; he became a bedwetter and his normally passive inclinations turned aggressive. She said he often came home from school wearing only one sock and he apparently could not have taken a nap because he would fall asleep in the car on the way home.

The mother said her three-year-old son masturbated "excessively" and sometimes used Vaseline and mayonnaise.

After his disclosures about the alleged abuse, the mother said the boy tried doing bizarre things to his body. Once when the mother was coming out of a shower, she testified her son tried to insert a nail file in her vagina. She said the boy was also fascinated by women with big breasts.

Cross-examination of the mother is expected to continue at 9 a.m.

Courtesy *The Star-Ledger.*

Detective quizzed in day-care sex abuse trial

*Defense tries to weaken credibility
of photos and children's testimony*

By Diane Curcio

Defense attorney Harvey Meltzer cross-examined a Maplewood police detective for three hours yesterday in Newark, focusing on pictures taken at the Wee Care Day Nursery and statements by children about alleged sexual abuse there.

Sorting through 25 photographs taken of the Maplewood nursery in May 1985, Meltzer questioned Detective Sgt. John J. Noonan about how he got into the building, the condition of the rooms and who was there.

Noonan explained that Diane Costa, a teacher in the defunct nursery, showed him and another investigator the nap rooms, where many children have alleged they were sexually abused.

Costa arranged the children's mats as they would have been during the school year, Noonan said, pointing out how he labeled the mats in the photographs. Meltzer asked if Costa knew which way the children were positioned—drawing objections from prosecutors.

Essex County Assistant Prosecutor Glenn D. Goldberg argued that the defense questioning was irrelevant "because there's no evidence" that any child could see what was happening on another child's mat.

Meltzer represents Margaret Kelly Michaels, 25, a one-time drama student, accused of sexually assaulting 20 boys and girls when she was a teacher at Wee Care.

Essex County Assistant Prosecutor Sara Sencer McArdle joined the arguments against Meltzer's cross-examination yesterday, contending there was no evidence that the children were victimized on mats.

Nineteen children have testified in the four-month-old case, detailing various sex acts, sometimes involving knives, forks and spoons, which allegedly took place during naptime and in the school bathrooms.

After more than 40 minutes of testimony on the mat photographs, Superior Court Judge William F. Harth said, "We're spending time out of all proportion. . . What's your next line of questioning?"

Meltzer then began quizzing Noonan on the statements made by three youngsters. Noonan either interviewed the children himself or was present when other investigators spoke with them.

Meltzer said later outside the courtroom that he focused on the children to show "inconsistencies and embellishments" between what the preschoolers told Noonan in June 1985 and their courtroom testimony.

For example, while one girl testified that she talked to Noonan about one type of sexual abuse, according to Meltzer, Noonan's reports showed her reporting another type.

Noonan said that after taking statements from some of the children and their parents, he and a partner drove the preschoolers to the day care center, where they showed police where the alleged assaults took place.

Meltzer asked if Noonan gave the youngsters toy badges that day and the detective said he did not recall. He testified previously that some Wee Care children had toured the police station in the wake of the investigation and badges then were distributed.

When the children visited Wee Care, accompanied by Noonan and other investigators, the youngsters showed police where they sat in the choir room. The choir room, which is also referred to as the music room or piano room by the youngsters, is where Michaels allegedly disrobed and played "Jingle Bells" on the piano, according to testimony. Children have also said they played a nude pileup game there.

Noonan took photographs of the children as they sat in the choir room pews. These and the other photographs of the facility were given to the jury late yesterday.

The trial is scheduled to reconvene at 9 a.m.

Courtesy *The Star-Ledger.*

CHAPTER 5

%%%%%%%%%%%%%%%%%%%%%%%%%%

Is It Logical?

- A union official claims that striking workers are paid an average of only $14,000 per year. You run that claim on a newscast; a company personnel manager calls you up and informs you that the striking workers make an average of $16,500. Is this logical? Can they both be right?

- A city official claims that senior citizens (diligent voters, by the way) are not a favored target for street criminals in a particular neighborhood. He argues that on a per capita basis other age groups in the neighborhood, such as teenagers, stand a greater chance of being victimized than do the elderly. Is this a logical conclusion?

- You are writing a magazine feature story on life expectancy. From actuarial tables, it is apparent that married men live longer than do single men. You see a catchy angle in the making: Loneliness Kills! Is this logical?

H.G. Wells, who was, among his other talents, a fine historian and something of a futurist, foresaw a day when statistical thinking would be as "necessary for efficient citizenship as the ability to read or write." And quite a powerful case could be made for statistical reasoning and logical analysis being just as important for the practicing journalist.[1]

---

1. Based on general readings of Wheeler (1976) and Engel (1986).

Discussion: Logical Fallacies and the Journalist

Journalists are frequently called on to sort out the ambiguous "average," such as in the first example above. Vested interests playing a numbers game might, as in the example, provide you with an "average." Note how the average salaries are plotted on the graph in figure 5.1. Point number 1 is the mode, or most frequently occurring salary. Point number 2 is the median, or that point in a distribution at which 50 percent are above and 50 percent are below. Point number 3 is the mean, the number you arrive at by adding together all the salaries and dividing by the total number of workers. All three are measures of what statisticians call *central tendency*. When push comes to shove in labor negotiations, each side may propose its own version of an "average" salary. Labor may quote modal salary ($14,000), while management may cite the mean salary ($16,500).

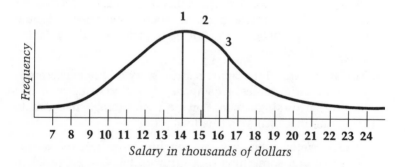

5.1. How three "averages" might be determined from one set of figures.

Proper definition is one key to avoiding logical pitfalls (and pratfalls). A reasonably informed understanding of how a statistic is derived is also critical. Take, for example, the politician who cited per capita (literally, "per head") figures to "prove" that the elderly were no more susceptible to crime than other groups. What he neglected to consider was the fact that the count of *all* the neighborhood's seniors included some who were institutionalized in a large nursing home and couldn't be street crime victims even if they wanted to be. The count also probably included a large number who were homebound or simply too terrified to venture out on the street.

Some other types of faulty reasoning prove dangerous for the reporter as well. Would you conclude in your magazine feature that loneliness kills[2] because actuarial statistics show that married men usually outlive single men? That's not a warranted assumption: while it *may* be true, it may also be false. In any event, such a premise cannot be concluded from an actuarial table which includes unmarried men who died in their teens from auto wrecks, young unmarried men drafted in preference to married men in wartime, and young men who suffered from terminal diseases and who were presumably less likely to marry even if they did reach marriage age.

Applying Logical Reasoning to Journalistic Decisions

Being aware of some fallacies most common to journalism can save you from embarrassment and possible legal action.

Cause and Effect Fallacy

The statistical linkage of two events does not necessarily mean that one caused the other, no matter how tantalizing the association. Unmarried men dying sooner than their married counterparts does not prove that loneliness kills. The presence of a rapist in an adult bookstore the morning before the rape does not *prove* that his exposure to pornography caused the rape. To use another simplified and rather simplistic example, natives of the New Hebrides once believed that body lice caused good health because

---

2. Example provided to the author by David Kleinke, associate professor of educational measurement, Syracuse University, for radio news program in 1979.

lice were never present on a sick individual. In truth, the phenomenon is explained by the fact that lice flee a feverish body.

Ignoring the Exposure Base

The politician who did not consider how many elderly were actually exposed to crime committed this fallacy. Again, to illustrate the concept with a simplistic example, assume that you're a fisherman and have a net with a six-inch mesh; in theory, the only fish you will see will be larger than six inches. If you conclude that all fish in the ocean are larger than six inches, you have ignored the fact that you have been exposed to a base made up of a biased sample.

Fallacies of Vacuity

Logician Robert J. Fogelin (1987, pp. 94–99) uses this category to sum up arguments which appear reasonable but are based on an unproven, empty (vacuous) assumption. *Circular reasoning* is one aspect of a fallacy of vacuity. A talk show guest, for example, may maintain that the draft is morally wrong, because it is wrong to force someone to join the army. But the argument is circular and hollow, because the guest is simply restating the initial conclusion: forcing someone to join the army *is* the draft.

An extension of circular reasoning is known as *begging the question*. In this case, the conclusion is, according to Fogelin, simply a "restatement of the conclusion in different words . . . used as a premise of the argument." For instance:

> It is always wrong to murder human beings.
> Capital punishment involves murdering human beings.
> Therefore, capital punishment is wrong. (p. 95)

What happens is this: the first statement reasonably appears to be true, since murder is defined as a wrongful killing. But the second statement calls capital punishment murder and uses that unproven and unsupported statement to "prove" a point.

Obviously many other logical fallacies exist, but it is beyond the scope of this work to examine formal logic to any great extent. There are some valuable books for journalists who wish to extend their skills in this area, and they are listed in the references of this work.

Checklist for Logical Analysis of News Items

The following points will serve as a general guide to keeping assumptions and reasoning on a logical plane.

1. Are the numbers provided meant to prove something? If so, be especially careful, for this is generally where half-truths and the whole truth part company. Question any figure that purports to make a case. If you are told that "revenues are up 20 percent," ask, "Up from what and when?"[3]

2. Does the story presume a cause and effect relationship? Far more serious than the "loneliness kills" fallacy is the example, cited in an earlier chapter, of the presumption that "people died in the fire because there were no smoke detectors."

3. Does the story or item reach for a spurious precision? If you are doing a piece on television viewing habits, and you poll three people who tell you they watch TV for "about two hours," "three hours," and "maybe three hours" per day, are you misleading your readers or viewers by stating that the average person watches TV for 2.666 hours per day? This is an extreme example, of course, but be cautious of any story construction that utilizes a precise-sounding number (which may be based on highly imprecise sampling).

4. Do your graphics mislead? Truncated bar graphs (graphs which only depict the top part of the graph, as shown in figure 5.2) can create an inaccurate impression of the numbers involved.

5. Do you (or people in your stories) present proof that does not really *prove* anything? Circular reasoning fallacies are one

---

3. Some of the best examples of seemingly worthwhile but basically worthless "proofs" are detailed by Rottenberg (1985), pp. 75–100.

example. Another is a vague statement to the effect that "Dr. Smith has proven that homosexuals are dangerous deviates." Who is Dr. Smith? What is he a doctor of? How did he "prove" this contention? Never let statements such as this pass unchallenged. Diligence is especially important in fast-moving media such as radio and television talk shows where charges are apt to be made irresponsibly by guests.[4]

Increase in Sales

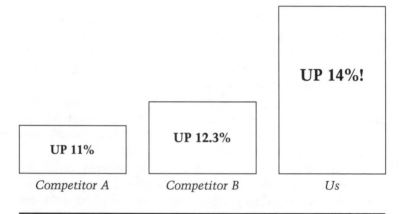

5.2.   Example of a misleading graph.

Case History: Of Violence and Victims

Reporters are often confronted with statistics related to crime. While it is beyond the scope of most news operations to mathematically analyze and verify those crime statistics, it is reasonable to expect a perceptive reporter to see if those numbers really prove something and to determine if there is sufficient reason to believe that the implied cause-and-effect relationship actually exists. (Note checklist items 1 and 2.)

That's exactly the task that WSM, Nashville, Radio News director

4. Illogical charges on talk shows are addressed by O'Donnell, Hausman, and Benoit (1987), p. 165.

Jerry Dahmen undertook in WSM's Peabody Award–winning 15-part radio series on the relationship of drugs to crime in Nashville. The series, reported by Dahmen, Liz White, and Dick Layman and engineered by Tom Bryant, closely examined Nashville's rising crime rate and scrutinized the purported cause-and-effect relationship between rising drug use and increasing crime rates.

In order to validate the drug-crime connection, Dahmen and his reporters spoke with addicts, police, and victims. Instead of merely accepting the established statistic that a high percentage of crime is

5.3   Jerry Dahmen, WSM, Nashville,
Radio News Director.

linked to drug use, WSM reporters interviewed victims of crime as well as addicts and users. In doing so, they accomplished two goals:

1. They brought crime figures "to life," so to speak, by showing that the numbers journalists so frequently encounter are, indeed, reflections of real human tragedy.

2. They showed, by speaking with the people who commit the crimes, that it is reasonable to assume that drugs are, indeed, responsible for a high percentage of the city's crime rate.

"We wanted to take those statistics and bring them to a people level," Dahmen explained. "And I came away from the series with the conclusion that drugs are a major part of the problem. I was surprised at how major the drug problem is; the series made me realize the tremendous cost of addiction and how far addicts and users would go to get the stuff."

Dahmen concludes with a point relevant to any newsperson working with numbers: "The firsthand evidence we obtained on the streets went right along with what the authorities were saying. We had no reason to disbelieve the crime statistics, but our investigation really brought the point home."

Here are some excerpts from the series. Some points to remember as you read them:

1. Note the inventive use of wild sound in the opening. It brings the point home and takes advantage of one of radio's underutilized strengths.

2. Examine the way that the crime-drug relationship is validated by several different people holding widely differing perspectives (a cop, a user, and a former user).

3. Notice how the interviews with addicts in parts two and three very clearly demonstrate that an addict has a great deal to gain from crime and very little compassion for his or her victim.

"Of Violence and Victims" Script—1

Excerpts from Part 1

NARRATOR: WSM Am News presents "Of Violence and Victims," the story of Nashville's rising tide of crime. Today, prevention and protection.

Extracts from "Of Violence and Victims," Parts 1, 2 and 3, courtesy WSM AM-FM, Nashville.

SOUND BITE: Woman screaming.

NARRATOR: Saturday night in General Hospital's emergency room . . . a woman in her 30s severely beaten by an attacker. Several days later, Davidson County's medical examiner conducts another autopsy—the victim of a brutal beating and stabbing.

MEDICAL EXAMINER: I'm preparing to remove the interior chest case so that we can see into the interior chest cavity.

SOUND BITE: Saw cutting through bone.

NARRATOR: If you think you're immune from violence, think again. Nashville's crime rate has increased 15 percent for the first half of this year compared with the first half of last year, and so have your chances of becoming a victim. These Nashvillians were probably like some of you. They knew about murder, stabbings, and robberies from listening to radio newscasts. That is, until they experienced them firsthand.

CRIME VICTIM: . . . a guy got killed . . . and that's it, OK? He got shot in the back of the head, and it came through his mouth.

CRIME VICTIM 2: The guy hit me, come very close to killing me, I jumped over a chain-link fence. I kicked the neighbor's door down to call the police. The guy's still in the house, he's got his ex-wife's kid, he kidnapped her kid . . .

[Segment continues with several additional eyewitness descriptions of very violent crimes.]

NARRATOR: Although we don't know the whys behind every crime, any metro vice officer will tell you drugs are the major factor behind them. Specifically, 75 to 80 percent are drug related. So what about these people who will harm your property, family, or you?

It didn't take very long to find several addicts and users in Nashville. When we did, they agreed to talk to us on the condition we changed their names. Jimmy is one of them.

JIMMY: I was sitting up on the pots and pans rack when he come over and stuck an icepick to my throat. He said, "I ought to stick you right now. Right when he said that I just kicked the [beep] out of him. I was up in the air, kinda like sitting, and I kicked him right in the damn jaw, knocked him back and the icepick went flying, so I jumped down on him and we started fighting real hard, and I got up and I said, "That guy's gonna actually try and kill me," so I grabbed a knife and run it down his back. I started at his neck and run it down almost to his butt. It was a real big long gash.

The Decision-Making Process in Journalism

NARRATOR: Shortly after one of our reporters met with Jimmy and his friends, I called ex-vice squad officer Thales Finchum, who told me whatever it takes to get their drugs, an addict or dealer will do it.

EX-VICE SQUAD OFFICER: Well they'll sell theirselves, they'll sell you, they'll sell their mother or their grandmother. In the end they'll do anything it takes to stay on the street and stay involved in drugs.

NARRATOR: Recently, a suspected cocaine user was arrested and charged with 50 Green Hills area burglaries. But, as you'll hear tomorrow, there are hundreds of other dealers and addicts who are still on the streets of music city—chomping at the bit to feed their habit at your expense and safety. I'm Jerry Dahmen, WSM Radio 650 News.

Excerpts from Part 2

BILLY (AN ADDICT): Oh, it makes me go off, and I just steal from my daddy, I steal from my mommy, I steal from my family, I steal from anybody I get my [beep] hands on and I don't give a [beep] about nobody.

NARRATOR: Billy has been wandering the streets most of her life. She ran away from home at the age of 10 and within a short time discovered drugs. Billy also learned how to get them.

BILLY: . . . and I loves my drugs and I go off into apartments and houses and [laughs] oh boy, it just makes me . . . I just loves it.

NARRATOR: One of Billy's street buddies is Jimmy. He's a 27-year-old Nashvillian whose career on dope started a decade ago.

JIMMY: I used to get it from a good friend of mine. That's back when I was going to school. I didn't have nothing else to do but party. So I'd go out, cut grass and stuff with a lawn mower, make me about $50 and I'd go buy some pills from him, take them, and sell them. That way I could make my profit and have my dope, too. And after I kept doing that so much, I had so much money between doing dope and cutting grass, I had like eight, nine pounds of pot, I had about 500 hits of mescaline, and tabs, and I had speed.

NARRATOR: The more he became involved in the drug business, the more Jimmy liked it. Money, and lots of it, became his addiction.

[Additional conversation with Jimmy, who details the easy profits available to drug dealers.]

Is It Logical?

NARRATOR: Jimmy is still on the streets selling and dealing. He doesn't care who gets hurt in the process. Neither do his customers. Gene is an ex-drug addict who got his act together after 25 years of using.

GENE: Many people have robbed their mothers, they've broken into their families' homes, stolen television sets, taken valuables and hocked them, only because they know their folks won't prosecute.

NARRATOR: And along the way, a lot of people get hurt. Some get killed. Metro vice squad officer Ryman Buchanan says the price of addiction isn't cheap in the 80s . . . and that's where the trouble starts.

VICE SQUAD OFFICER: You take a person who wakes up in the morning and they know, well, "I've got a $500" or "a $2,000 a day" habit, every day, 365 days a year. "Where am I going to get the money?" And they get to panicking. They are going to get that money for the drugs somehow or other, or they're going to get some drugs, if they have to steal to get the money to get the drugs, or if they have to rip somebody off to get the drugs, they're going to get the drugs—that comes first.

NARRATOR: The drug addicts we talked to agreed with Buchanan. They told us about a product on the marketplace that is worth the risk of getting stabbed, shot, or put behind bars: Cocaine. Billy and Danny, both users, say it's the ultimate trip.

[Interview with Billy and Danny, who describe their attraction to cocaine and their willingness to do anything to get the drug.]

Excerpts from Part 3

NARRATOR: Most of us think about our families and friends. We have compassion, love, and a sense of humanity. But for drug dealers in Nashville like Jimmy, their minds are obsessed with one commodity: money. It's a business that one dealer says is the best investment in the world. As he put it, "where else can you take $1 million and have 30 times that amount in 30 days without paying taxes?" But when you're dealing with drugs, keep this in mind: Be willing to do whatever it takes to bring in the cash.

[Interviews with dealers and users who talk about their crimes, describing their lack of concern about danger and total absence of compassion for their victims.]

CHAPTER 6

❧❧❧❧❧❧❧❧❧❧❧❧❧❧❧❧❧❧❧❧❧❧❧❧

Is It Distorted?

Marshall McLuhan theorized that "the medium *is* the message," referring to the interrelation between the message itself and the way it is presented by the media—the fact that the carrier influences the idea far more than might be imagined. There is relevance in that observation for the news reporter, because the trappings of a particular media may often alter the meaning of what is being reported.

For example:

- You are interviewing someone for a television news magazine program. He freely admits wrongdoing in what is a relatively casual conversation before your remote camera. At the conclusion of the interview, the camera is turned on you so that you may re-ask the questions, which will be edited into the final tape. This time, you adopt a harsh, accusatory tone. When the piece is edited and aired, it appears as though you browbeat the information out of the guest.

Is this a serious distortion?

- During research for a newspaper story, you interview a colorful Southern politician, Politician A. He provides you with quotes such as, "When you deal with Politician B, you have to stomp your foot a few times to get him to crawl back under his rock . . . always works." Politician B, who is on the other side of the issue, is a quiet and colorless man who speaks without elaboration but does address the facts. The story, thick with quotes from Politician A, reads beautifully, but Politician B is virtually ignored.

Have you distorted the issue?

- As a producer for an evening TV newscast, you are assigned to cover the drug situation at a local college campus. You would like to film a pot party; an acquaintance who attends the college tells you he can arrange one.

Will you distort the story by indirectly taking part in arranging the pot party?

These questions reflect a type of decision faced on virtually a daily basis by journalists: Where does the message end and the medium take over?

Keeping Distortion in Proportion

The first example, the TV cutaway shot, is an easily grasped case of how the visual requirements of the medium can, indeed, distort the message. Most television interviews done on location are taped with one camera, but this leaves a visual "hole" which the viewer wants to see filled. The viewer naturally wants to see the person asking the question, as would be the case in normal conversation. The so-called "reverse shot" is also used for the convenience of the editor, since the reverse shot can be used to piece together parts of the interview without a "jump cut." A jump cut is a sudden movement of the subject when a portion of the tape is edited out and the remaining segments pieced together.

Motivations of reporters differ, but it is not unheard of for a television reporter to feel as though he or she would benefit from having the reputation and appearance of a tough investigator who extracts the truth from an unwilling guest. It seems clear that this type of re-taping and editing indeed is a distortion, and the practice has attracted some attention in the industry.

CBS news producer Sanford Socolow, for several years the executive producer of "The CBS Evening News with Walter Cronkite," favors the use of jump cuts instead of cutaways. He has been quoted as maintaining that jump cuts are "more honest" because the viewer knows that something has been chopped out of the interview."[1]

There is really no universal agreement on the use of cutaways and reversals, just as there is no standard formula for making quotes fairly reflect the issues at hand. It is an unfortunate fact of life (unfortunate from the writer's point of view) that some people can communicate in "news-speak" while others cannot. The news-speak communicator uses bite-size ideas and colorful, quotable language. Those who have not mastered the tongue often express their ideas in drab language and give answers which are long and difficult to edit, either for TV or print.

Just as print relies on colorful quotes, TV relies on evocative pictures. This, of course, creates many a dilemma for a reporter needing video to back up his or her story. Such was the case in November 1966, when station WBBM-TV in Chicago aired two news segments entitled "Pot Party at a University."[2] A cooperative contact arranged for a reporter to attend a pot party, and eventually it was arranged that the party be filmed. Later investigation revealed the reporter had paid the participants $5 after, the reporter maintains, an indignant party-goer badgered him into the payment.

The pot party, ostensibly on the campus of Northwestern University (there was some confusion as to whether the location actually was on university-owned property) touched off a furor. Hearings were held on the now-classic case, inquiring as to whether the station had "set up" the party in the interests of sensationalism or possibly to "get" the university.

In the end, an FCC hearing examiner concluded that the pot party was indeed prearranged for the cameras. The station was chastised and ordered to set up responsible guidelines for the news department, but no action was taken against the station's license.

Plainly, each of the three problems—cutway shots, colorful quotes, and presence of a camera—has no clear-cut solution, although strong cases could be made and have been made that each involves an unacceptable distortion. But because distortion

1. Quoted by White et al. (1984), p. 193.

2. Discussed at length in Sandman, Rubin, and Sachsman (1977), pp. 83–95.

is by nature often difficult to detect, and because circumstances vary so widely case by case, the journalist usually deals with the issue by application of his or her own standards.

Applying Standards to Issues of Distortion

As an example, WFAA-TV (Dallas) investigative reporter Byron Harris avoids the use of stand-up tags during his report. A stand-up tag is the concluding remark the reporter makes to the camera after the piece is through. It is almost always given with the subject of the report (a fire scene, perhaps, or the state Capitol) in the background. Harris feels the stand-up tag is a clear distortion of the report.

> Print reporters never had to write the last paragraph of a story before they write the story. TV reporters do it all the time. That's what a stand-up is. And that's an incredible thing. It's the essence: We're going to make you decide, out in the field, after being on this story for an hour, what the final line is going to be. And you're locked into that. That's absurd.[3]

Journalists also tend to be wary of the person who is fluent in news-speak or the organization which makes a point of manufacturing news. Public relations practitioners are adept at putting the news in a package which can be used easily by the media. In fact, critic and analyst Herbert J. Gans, who undertook an extensive study on how news *becomes* news, maintains that if the relationship between journalists and sources is a dance, it is usually the sources who lead.[4] They make themselves available, keep in contact, put forth story ideas, and in practice "manage the news by putting the best light on themselves."

"Selling to the media" relates to distortions caused by media's requirements. TV and newspapers need pictures; radio needs tape recordings of newsmakers and events. Sophisticated public

3. See Biagi (1987), p. 204.
4. Paraphrased by Turk (1986), p. 4.

relations experts often provide prepackaged radio and television spots for use by the media. Many public relations agencies seeking to place stories in newspapers send appealing photos with the press release.

Obviously, it is incumbent on journalists not to make their selections based on the slickness of the public relations effort, but convenience can and does play a part in the hectic operations of a newsroom. Journalists must use their judgment in order to avoid being manipulated by the packager of easy-to-use news.

Likewise, they must avoid distorting the presentation in such a way as to manipulate the readers or audience. While it is reasonable to assume that few journalists intentionally use the trappings of the media to sway readers, viewers, or listeners to a particular point of view, such a distortion-based bias can be unconscious on the part of the newscaster or imagined on the part of the audience. The author, for example, a former TV newscaster, was once criticized by more than a dozen telephone callers following a newscast for his "disapproving look" when reading a story about a local candidate. The "disapproving look," in point of fact, was indicative only of a toothache.

What have become known as "raised eyebrow" complaints (complaints relating to a newscaster's expression) typically are all that more baffling because they often involve a viewer's misreading of an expression. But there may be some evidence to suggest that newscaster expressions do affect perception. A study published in 1986, for example, purported to demonstrate that test subjects were able to detect positive facial expressions on the part of newscasters and would likely base their voting more on the newscaster's expression than on the content of the story.[5] (Peter Jennings, for example, was alleged to exhibit a strong positive bias in favor of Ronald Reagan.)

In summary, unintended distortions can change the message. It is just as important for a reporter to guard against *accidental* distortion as against purposeful distortion. Both alter the meaning and message. Meaning and message are also altered by distortions affecting the information before it reaches the audience,

---

5. See Mullen et al. (1986).

such as public relations inspired stories or stories enhanced by the addition of visuals or other conveniences.

Criteria: Is It Distorted?

When trying to gauge whether such distortions have affected your work or your news judgment, the following questions may be helpful:

1. Is my use of the story a matter of convenience? If the same union official calls to offer comment on a situation each day—and you record and use his statement because you are hungry for taped segments in your radio newscast—convenience may have come at the price of distortion.

Your coverage may lack balance because you overload newscasts with interviews fed to you in a convenient manner. The same problem might arise if, for example, a public relations firm arranges for the firm's clients to visit your studio at your convenience and tape news interviews. The end result might be that you are overloading your news with public-relations inspired interviews simply because the PR firm made things easy for you. Consider these points when choosing and using news items, and guard against convenience-inspired distortion.

Use of previously discussed "composite quotes" is an example of possible convenience-inspired distortion. It is much easier to make up the exact wording you want and attribute it to a "composite" of characters[6] than to work with the material at hand. Guard against this type of laziness.

2. Am I directly changing events or causing events to happen by my presence? There are no hard-and-fast rules, but most experienced journalists advise that the line be drawn at the point where presence of a reporter *causes something to happen because of a direct or indirect request by the reporter.* For example, the arrival of a television truck will certainly motivate picketers to resume their positions at the line. That is probably

---

6. For further discussion of how the composite character question is affecting journalism, see Stephens (1981), p. 13.

inevitable, and it seems clear that there is no true distortion in using this tape. The picketers took the line of their own free will, and what happened reflects a real and ongoing situation. However, if the picketers were eating dinner at a restaurant across the street and the reporter *asked* them to return to the line, most journalists would regard that as a distortion. The pot-party case would seem to indicate the same clear principle: If you come across a pot party and want to film it, fine; if you *arrange* a pot party so you can get some good pictures, you're in the wrong.

3. Have technical factors related to the media altered my news judgment? A story overloaded with good quotes from a proponent of one side of the issue *is* distorted. Like it or not, you must balance it, even if that means cutting some of the colorful quotes and paraphrasing a portion of the unusable material from the dull bureaucrat. And while good pictures will always be important to TV and good interviews critical to radio, do not entirely base your story selection on those points. Make a conscious effort to utilize important stories even if they are not "naturals" for the medium.

4. Has editing changed the context of my material? As illustrated, cutaway shots can change the viewer's impression of what actually happened if those shots are edited in a careless or deceptive way. Print editing, too, can change context. Remember, even a reporter "edits" to an extent because he or she cannot use all the material available. Be sure your selection process does not isolate facts or statements out of context.

Case History: Bumpers v. Clark

"Politicians are marvelous distorters," according to Paul F. Parsons, a former UPI and AP reporter who currently is the R.M. Seaton Professional Journalist at Kansas State University. "They can take complex issues and turn them into [simplistic] one- or two-sentence descriptions. Also, they can dredge up peripheral issues attached to political actions, such as passage of a certain bill which had riders attached to it and distort the whole issue."

Parsons found himself covering an emotion-laden story when Bill Clark squared off against Dale Bumpers in a hotly contested race for

U.S. Senate. "I had to tread very carefully," Parsons recalled, "in order to write a balanced article."

In other words, Parsons was wading into a minefield of emotional issues, charges, and countercharges—and had to present a balanced view to his readers.

What were his most immediate problems?

1. "In my desire to be fair, and to tell both sides, I first had to develop a proper lead. [Author's note: by a proper lead, Parsons meant one which did not distort the issues by raising an unimportant piece of information to great importance by virtue of running it first in the story, a concept discussed earlier in this chapter.] I felt that Bill Clark's allegations about the incumbent were the most newsworthy pieces of information, and I made a conscious decision to make those charges the focus of the story."

2. "I had to make sure readers would not think I was advocating what Clark was saying. A journalist does that by building in the other side as high as possible into the story, so that readers can see that there's a dispute here. Readers will also see, I hope, that the journalist is trying to tell both sides."

Notice these constructs as you read the story.

Note, too, that Parsons did manage to sift out a fair account of the bitter race. As a sidelight, Parsons recalled that after the story appeared, Clark's aide called to tell Parsons, in effect, that the story had really exposed Bumpers "as the liberal he is." Parsons was quite disturbed by that call—thinking he'd inadvertently written a pro-Clark story—until several hours later, when a Bumpers aide called to thank Parsons for exposing *Clark.*

Clark Fight To Unseat Bumpers
Using Religion As Big Gun

LITTLE ROCK (AP)—It's just the beginning of October, and already Sen. Dale Bumpers (D-Ark.) has been called a hypocrite, a liar and an incompetent by his Republican opponent, Bill Clark.

Clark certainly hasn't hesitated to bring out the heavy artillery early. He's far behind in the polls, and his only hope to unseat Bumpers from the U.S. Senate after one term is to convince voters this is a classic confrontation between a liberal and a conservative.

Clark, who ran unsuccessfully as a conservative Democrat for Congress four years ago, has leveled these charges against Bumpers in recent weeks:

• He said at the opening of his state campaign headquarters in June that Bumpers "has always run on style, not substance; on his shoeshine and smile, as the saying goes."

• He told a Republican gathering in Little Rock that Bumpers "is not competent enough" to be a U.S. senator, and cited Bumpers' vote in favor of the Panama Canal treaties and Bumpers' support for the SALT 2 treaty as evidence.

• He said in Russellville on July 21 that Bumpers is a "hypocrite" who "has lied to the voters" by masking his liberal leanings during the re-election campaign.

• Speaking in Brinkley, Clark said the federal government "seems determined to put our farms out of business and Dale Bumpers consistently votes in support of that policy, against the farmers."

• Clark told the Benton County Republican Convention that Bumpers is too liberal to be a "fit representative" for the people of Arkansas and that "you can't believe a word Bumpers says."

• Clark told the Central Church of the Nazarene in Little Rock on a Sunday morning that Bumpers is not providing moral leadership in Washington, adding, "He does, in fact, act one way on Sunday morning in church and another way on the floor of the Senate."

Clark has called his anti-Bumpers rhetoric "an informative campaign, not a dirty campaign." However, Bumpers said Clark is running a "repugnant" campaign based on personal attacks.

This has become a year in which conservative Christian groups have become politically active nationwide. Arkansas is no exception, and Clark predicts he will receive the religious vote in November.

"Dale has voted 23 times for taxpayer funding of abortions. This is wrong," Clark said. "Most of the people who believe in that believe in euthanasia. The elderly are concerned about this.

"I wish Dale Bumpers had voted properly most of the time. I would be the first to say, 'Hey, stay up there and do a good job.' But he has taken a very anti-Arkansas record.

"I'm not attacking Dale Bumpers personally, but I'm saying his voting record shows a lack of concern about moral issues such as school prayer," Clark said. "I'm merely relaying information to the people."

In his talk to the Little Rock church, Clark cited a moral issues rating given to U.S. senators by The Christian Voice, a national political lobby.

Bumpers scored an 8 per cent in the rating, compared to a 92 per cent rating for Rep. Ed Bethune and a 100 per cent rating for Rep. John Paul Hammerschmidt (both R-Ark.)

Bumpers dismissed the rating as meaningless. He said an Alabama congressman who is a Baptist preacher scored a 13 per cent, and Sen. John Glenn (D-Ohio)—"a Presbyterian elder and one of the most devout men I have ever known"—scored zero.

"I saw where Ronald Reagan met with fundamentalist preachers in Dallas," Bumpers said. "Sometimes it can get a bit scary because the Constitution says there shall be no religious tests for holding office.

"People expect their public officials to be men with a church background, actively involved in church work, and so on. I don't see anything wrong with that. But when you start demanding a litmus test on doctrinaire questions, that poses a problem."

Clark sees the Senate race as being closely aligned to the Carter-Reagan race in Arkansas. "I think the people of Arkansas consider the President to be a Christian man," he said. "He's just incompetent. He can't handle the job. And Dale Bumpers has been supporting him and his program. What does that say about Dale Bumpers?

"This is a classic confrontation between a conservative and a liberal," Clark said. "I don't mind being called a conservative. Dale obviously does mind being called a liberal. I read where he called himself a conservative. I say hogwash to that. He's going to have to run on his voting record and his label—a liberal. I'm not going to let him get over here on the conservative side."

Bumpers said he believes some of Clark's comments have gotten out of hand.

"Voters respond more to a positive approach and one that expresses hope for the future rather than those personal vendettas," Bumpers said. "I think that sort of campaign is not only repugnant to the voters, but I think it demeans their intelligence. The voters have a very good ability to separate the chaff from the wheat."

Clark said the attacks will continue because voters need to know of Bumpers' liberal voting record. Bumpers, meanwhile, is staying quiet with what he believes to be a comfortable lead, and says he will remain "thick-skinned" in the final month of the campaign.

Courtesy The Associated Press.

CHAPTER 7

᪥᪥᪥᪥᪥᪥᪥᪥᪥᪥᪥᪥᪥᪥᪥᪥᪥᪥᪥᪥᪥᪥

Is It Libelous or an Invasion of Privacy?

Libel and privacy are two of the most confusing areas of the American legal system (which is not known for simplicity and clarity). And to be realistic, the only safe assumption in this area is the idea that simplistic definitions of libel and privacy and narrow examples of how related laws are applied would probably do more harm than good.

Why? Because those laws change with the seeming irregularity of New England weather, and their applications vary from state to state. To make matters more complex, the interpretation of libel—how much leash journalists have at any particular time— is often determined by the pendulumlike swings of court interpretation of existing statutes.[1]

Discussion: The Fundamentals of Libel and Privacy Laws

Because of the nebulous and fluid nature of the law, this chapter will serve more as an indicator of when you should ask for help (from your newspaper or station's lawyer, or from senior news executives) than a guide for precise determination of the risk of litigation. Knowing where, when, and how the red flags are raised can save you embarrassment and considerable anguish.

---

1. An excellent summary of the ebb and flow of media law is provided by Seeger (1987).

Libel: Definition and Defense

Libel is defined in many ways, and no definition is all-encompassing.[2] One of the better definitions is supplied by journalism professor Martin L. Gibson (1979) of the University of Texas, Austin:

> Libel is defined as the publication of any representation that tends to hold a person up to hatred, contempt, or ridicule; that causes him to be shunned or lose respect; or that harms him or his occupation. (p. 188)

Gibson also notes that the concept is easier to understand if you consider the fact that any defamation (statement that damages or tarnishes one's reputation) becomes libel when it is an *unjust* defamation.

Implicit in the above definition of libel are several requirements, that is, conditions that must be fulfilled before a libel is committed. To expand on the definition of libel, then, the requirements are:

1. *Publication.* The libel must be transmitted to a third party via publication. In legal terminology, "publication" refers to broadcasting a libelous statement, as well as publishing it in print.

2. *Damage.* It must be shown in court that the person charging libel actually was harmed by the published statement; that, for example, his or her reputation was harmed or source of income was damaged.

3. *Identification.* There must be proof that the person claiming libel can actually be linked to the alleged libel; that is, if a mention appears about a "dishonest movie theater owner on 42nd Street," (hypothetical example) is there sufficient evidence in the article or story to single out a particular theater owner?

---

2. Discussion of libel requirements and defenses reflects standard industry knowledge, but some points are drawn from Gibson (1979), pp. 187–198, White et al. (1984), pp. 54–55, and Metzler (1986), pp. 255–273.

Be aware that any representation can constitute a libel, including a photo or a description which identifies a person without using his or her name.

4. *Fault.* In order for a libel case to be won by a defendant, it must be proven that the reporter involved was in some way at fault. Publishing an incorrect statement is an obvious example. But when the plaintiff (the one who sues the reporter) is a public figure, a person who has thrust himself or herself into the limelight, an additional measure of fault must be proven. In general, it must be shown that the reporter acted with *actual malice* when publishing false information about a public figure.

There are four primary defenses against libel. (Others exist, and there are many permutations of libel defense, but for general purposes the following provide a reasonable scope of understanding.)

1. *Demonstrable truth.* Bear in mind that "truth" is not quite the same thing as "demonstrable truth." A reporter must prove a statement in court in order to use this defense against libel, and that is not always easy. It may very well be true that the subject of your story is a "mobster," but how can that be proved?

2. *Privilege.* The American system of government holds that a free and open debate is necessary for the workings of democracy and as such gives absolute protection against libel for remarks made on the floor of a legislative body while that body is in session, or to remarks made in court while court is in session.

A reporter can repeat such remarks without fear of being sued for libel as long as he or she gives an accurate and balanced reporting. This type of privilege is usually known as "qualified privilege." Qualified privilege means, for example, that you are safe from libel if you report what would be slanderous remarks made by a witness during a trial *as long as you make a good faith effort to report the balancing testimony.*

Qualified privilege also applies to fair and accurate reportings of official government actions, such as the arrest of suspects. It is important to note that reports of arrest are frequently the subject of libel suits, although almost always as a result of a factual error in reporting or the direct implication that the person arrested *committed* the crime, as opposed to *being charged* with the crime.

3. *Fair comment.* This defense holds, in effect, that someone has a right to express an opinion about issues which interest others. Fair comment protection, though, extends only as far as the direct issue at hand. You cannot be sued for a scathing review of a restaurant, for example, unless you make flagrantly fraudulent claims. You cannot be sued for a derogatory remark about an actor's performance, but you do have some libel exposure if you make untrue allegations about the actor's private life. Likewise, you cannot be held liable for a product review unless you make what are deemed to be fraudulent or misleading statements in the review.

4. *Public figure.* The landmark case *Times v. Sullivan* held that people who thrust themselves into the public eye forfeit some of their protection against being libeled. Briefly, *Times v. Sullivan* involved a southern police commissioner who sued *The New York Times* because the *Times* printed (in an advertisement carried but not originally composed by the newspaper) some allegedly libelous remarks about the commissioner's treatment of blacks. The U.S. Supreme Court held in 1964 that, because of the fact that our society cherishes free and open discourse, a public official exposes himself or herself to public criticism and must, in order to collect damages, prove that "a defamatory statement was made with actual malice, that is, with knowledge that it was false or with reckless disregard of whether it was false or not."

The trend of court cases in the decade following *Times v. Sullivan* would broaden the scope of a public official to include that of a public figure.

Privacy Invasion: Definition and Defenses

Journalists encounter libel suits far more frequently than privacy suits, or threats of privacy suits, but the danger exists nonetheless. Perhaps more importantly, there is a basic principle of decency included here, because privacy issues often involve people who have done nothing to thrust themselves into the public eye and ostensibly do not have the capability to defend themselves against being portrayed in an unfair light. For example, a person well established as a public figure (a movie star, for example) has ample access to the media should he or she wish to counter reporting which that person considers damaging. A private person does not.

Do those people who lead basically private lives have a right to damages if a reporter digs into embarrassing details of his or her past? Generally, the courts hold that they do.

While there is no clear-cut definition of invasion of privacy, you can generally assume that you will invade someone's privacy if you thrust an essentially private person into the public eye in such a way that he or she is embarrassed or portrayed in a false light. You also are invading someone's privacy if you use unreasonable measures to thrust yourself (and by extension, the public) into that person's private area. You cannot trespass on private property, even on a public figure's property, and you cannot carry journalistic observation to the point of harassment.

If the definition seems vague, it is. It can only reflect what appear to be, at the time of this writing, the most palpable legal trends in this very complex issue.

Along the same lines, there are few clearly defined defenses against invasion of privacy, although the following two principles are reasonable criteria.

1. *Consent of the subject.* Someone who willingly gives you details of his or her private life will have little recourse when those facts are published. A guest on a talk show will sacrifice much of his or her right to privacy and will have a difficult (but probably not impossible) case to make in proving invasion of privacy if the talk turns to embarrassing details of his or her private life. Even being on a public street implies the subject's consent, to a degree. A man walking down the street arm in arm with a woman who was not his wife would have little recourse for an invasion of privacy suit if the photo taken of them were run in a matter not misleading to the reader.

2. *Willing or unwilling involvement of the subject in an incident of public record.* Someone participating in a demonstration can be photographed and/or identified. Someone who is thrust

into a news event, such as a man shot down on the street, is part of an event of public interest and record and can be identified without recourse to a privacy action.

Certain categories of crime victims, though, are provided explicit privacy protections under various laws, such as the prohibition against publishing the names of sex-crime victims. A recent case chipped away slightly at the laws that prohibit such publications, but only in a very narrow circumstance. The case, *Florida Star v. B.J.F.*, involved a small Jacksonville, Florida, paper which printed the name of a rape victim. The name inadvertently had been provided by police to a reporter/trainee at the *Star* and used—against the paper's policy—in a crime story.

There is a Florida criminal law against the publication of a rape victim's name, and although the case was not pressed as a criminal action, B.J.F. (the initials of the victim) filed a civil privacy and negligence suit. The state appeals court upheld damages for $97,500.

However, the U.S. Supreme Court in the summer of 1989 reversed that decision, holding that it is a violation of the First Amendment to punish a newspaper for printing information legally obtained. That decision, though, was drawn so narrowly that it may, for all intents and purposes, apply only to *Florida Star v. B.J.F.* According to an accounting of the decision in *Editor & Publisher*, Justice Thurgood Marshall, who wrote the majority opinion, emphasized that the court did *not* hold: (1) that true accounts are automatically constitutionally protected; (2) that states cannot protect personal privacy from press intrusion; (3) that states cannot punish publication of names of sex-crime victims.[3]

Application of Libel and Privacy Laws to the Business of Journalism

In all candor, it is impossible to gain a comprehensive understanding of libel and privacy laws through a single chapter or

---

3. Summary from *Editor & Publisher* (July 1, 1989), pp. 10, 11.

Is It Libelous or an Invasion of Privacy?

even a course in media law. Some would argue that with the current state of such laws, even a judge may be confused—and that is exactly the sentiment aired by former Philadelphia Court Judge Lois G. Forer in a broadcast interview.[4]

> ... no one really knows what the law of libel is today. We see these ridiculous verdicts of millions of dollars for people who at the most have suffered hurt feelings.... The law is different in all fifty states, and plaintiffs are jurisdiction-shopping all over the country to find the jurisdiction that is most favorable.... What has happened is this chilling effect for all publications.

And that chilling effect cuts directly to the heart of current debate over libel laws. As Judge Forer noted:

> Now, almost every major publisher and electronic media has a lawyer sitting in the offices—editorial offices—vetting the news. There is this cautiousness that is preventing the public from getting the information it needs.... This is really a shocking perversion of the First Amendment.

It seems clear that the legal quagmire of libel, and to a lesser extent, privacy laws, is indeed resulting in what is effectively prior restraint. A survey conducted during a convention of a group known as Investigative Reporters and Editors (IRE) found that more than half of the respondents said that the concern over libel had some effect on journalistic decisions involving what they covered and how they covered it.[5]

Even though the media win an estimated 90 percent of libel cases, the defendant still must bear the cost of the defense, which can be crushingly high. In recent years, there have been several cases where this threat—the threat of court costs paid even if the case is won—has purportedly caused various media to back

---

4. Quotes taken verbatim from interview on CNN television network, December 14, 1987.

5. Reported by Labunksi, R.E. and Pavlik, J.V. (1986).

away from stories,[6] although on occasion executives of the media involved have claimed that the threat of libel had nothing to do with the decision not to publish. Cases of apparent restraint due to threat of litigation have extended to articles in major magazines and books under contract to major publishers.

The changing nature of damage awards further complicates the issue. A case involving *Hustler* magazine publisher Larry Flynt and the Reverend Jerry Falwell originally seemed to extend a legal remedy to those whose feelings are hurt.[7] The case involved a parody of a liquor ad in which the Reverend Falwell was portrayed as, among other things, being an incestuous drunkard. The "advertisement" was clearly satire, albeit tasteless and crude, and the jury in *Falwell v. Flynt* found that Falwell had not been libeled since no reasonable reader would assume the advertisement was true. But the jury did award Falwell $200,000 for "emotional distress."

For the time being, though, it appears that the so-called "distress call" is not sufficient for awarding of libel damages, because in early 1988 the U.S. Supreme Court reversed the original decision. Chief Justice William Rehnquist wrote that the parody was "doubtless gross and repugnant in the eyes of most," but also noted that the First Amendment protects "vehement, caustic and sometimes unpleasantly sharp attacks" against public figures.[8]

This decision extends the protection offered the media under *Times v. Sullivan.* The legal theory essentially says that the statement at issue was not made with "reckless disregard" for the truth because, according to Justice Rehnquist, the parody "was not reasonably believable" and was therefore considered satire and allowed considerably more leeway.[9]

6. For information on two recent cases, see "Author regains rights" (1987), and "Threat of suit" (1985).

7. Some details drawn from James J. Kilpatrick (1987) syndicated column in the *Worcester* (MA) *Telegram.*

8. Quote from *Newsweek* (March 7, 1988), p. 8.

9. From *U.S. News & World Report* (March 7, 1988), pp. 11, 12.

Many observers note that this is the latest swing of the pendulum away from what might be called "pseudolibel"—suits that extend the boundaries of traditional claims.

Recent privacy case decisions are changing the playing field, too. The U.S. Supreme Court let stand a lower court decision that an unwed teenage father's privacy had been invaded because he was identified in an article *even though he consented to the interview.*[10] The crux of the matter appeared to be the fact that the subject was a minor at the time of the interview. Effects of the ruling on future privacy cases are unclear.

Criteria: Checklist for Avoiding Libel and Privacy Actions

If nothing else, the foregoing discussion makes it painfully obvious that cookbook formulae for avoidance of libel and privacy actions are worthless at best, dangerous at worst. That's why the "red flag" approach seems the most reasonable and useful.

Following are questions to consider; if they raise any red flags, consult with legal counsel or senior news executives at your newspaper, magazine, publisher, or broadcast or cable station. In all decision-making, refer to the general principles and discussion presented up to this point. The following checklist presents *particular* areas which often prove dangerous because they reflect an unexpected opportunity for a libel or privacy suit—and many cases do arise from "back door" or "accidental" libel.

1. Does my story contain anything potentially damaging to someone's business? It appears to some reporters that subjects can withstand a reasonable amount of damage to their reputations and egos, but when the pocketbook is threatened, the lawsuits start to fly. Be exceptionally cautious about any reference which could be construed as an attack on business practices. Such statements may not be obvious libels, but they can and do wind up in court.

---

10. Covered in "Award for name use" (1987), p. 25.

2. Does my story focus unflatteringly, and perhaps inadvertently, on *an individual?* Many libel situations evolve when a discussion of a general condition (for example, shoddy car-repair practices) is linked, purposely or by accident, to an individual (a video cover shot of a particular person's repair shop). While groups can sue for libel, they rarely do so. *Individuals* sue for libel in the overwhelming majority of cases. So while a piece which finds fault with an entire profession (doctors, lawyers, repair-people) may not be actionable, a deliberate or inadvertent reference to a single, identifiable person may be.

3. Is there any question as to the accuracy and completeness of facts relating to an arrest? Are addresses complete and accurate? Is the charge correct? Many libel cases stem from slip-ups in handling of names, whereby the wrong person is accidentally identified. Other problems arise when the reporter makes an inaccurate conclusion from the facts. John Doe may have been arrested in a drug raid, *but he is not necessarily charged with drug possession.* Be sure that you know for a fact that possession charges have been lodged before you report this. Finally, be certain that your wording is crystal clear when discussing the charges. You must always say, for example, that "police charged John Doe with child molestation," and not conclude that "John Doe was arrested after he molested a child."

4. Is there any way that a person could construe his or her mention or image as being embarrassing or putting him or her in a false light? For example, one editor (in a case which is still under litigation and cannot be discussed in precise detail) used a silhouette from a wedding photo in a stylized way to illustrate a story on divorce. The woman pictured, still married, claimed that she was identifiable from the silhouette and further claimed that many of her friends had called her to express shock and amazement at her divorce. She filed suit. The lesson: Consider each case from all possible angles and points of view.

5. In any and all cases, triple check the relationship of names to facts; a haphazard linkage is where a great many libel cases originate. If you are writing an article about the poor design of a building, for example, be sure that the name of any architect mentioned be clearly placed within the proper context of the

story. A casual reference to an architect who may have been involved in another phase of the design (not related to the faults cited in the article) could result in litigation if there is any possibility that the story could be interpreted as incorrectly faulting the architect for the shoddy work. Remember: *Names should raise flags—always.*

Case History: Liberty Lobby v. Dow Jones

While no one would argue that libel laws are not well-intentioned, there is a considerable case to be made that the laws may have a chilling effect on press coverage. Reporters may be afraid to report because they fear litigation.

But won't justice win out if the facts are on the reporter's side? Not always. The following case history, recounted by a veteran legal reporter, shows how *The Wall Street Journal* found itself winning a libel case but still losing.

Libel: Losing While Winning

By Lyle Denniston

Every now and then, a court case comes along to remind the press that libel law remains a mess and that reform is long overdue. The latest reminder comes in a case that probably should never have been allowed in court at all, yet it took more than three years to wend its way to inevitable defeat.

The case was a thoroughly routine one, with no chance of setting any new precedents to guide the press and its adversaries in their continuing combat over defamation law. But the case attracted a little more than routine attention because it was the "swan song" of Judge Robert H. Bork, the last significant opinion the defeated Supreme Court nominee would write before quitting the federal bench to return to legal scholarship and public debate over the nature of law in America.

Bork's fame, though, is beside the point in this instance. The case deserves close study by the press because it illustrates so well the depths to which libel litigation has fallen.

Reprinted courtesy *Washington Journalism Review*.

7.1   Lyle Denniston, *The Baltimore Sun.*

Nearly 24 years after the Supreme Court sought (in *New York Times v. Sullivan*) to liberate the press so that it could report more freely on public affairs and public figures, the case of *Liberty Lobby v. Dow Jones* offers clear proof that *Sullivan* was not true to its promise. In fact, Liberty Lobby, a publishing organization that operates on the far fringes of the right wing, has proved repeatedly over the years that it can make the press pay dearly—in both legal and pure nuisance costs—for the victory the press supposedly won in the 1964 *Sullivan* ruling. As Judge Bork wrote in the latest Liberty Lobby case, "The message to . . . the press at large is clear: discussion of Liberty Lobby is expensive." He noted that litigation "can be very expensive if not crippling."

Liberty Lobby has made something of a habit of suing other publishers, and writers, for libel. Beginning about 15 years ago, the organization has sued six different times, always against someone who had suggested that Liberty Lobby was either racist, anti-Semitic, or both. Among its other targets have been the late columnist, Drew Pearson; Pearson's successor, Jack Anderson; and *National Review* magazine and its publisher, William F. Buckley. Not once has Liberty Lobby won such a case and, in fact, every one has been thrown out without ever reaching a jury.

Is It Libelous or an Invasion of Privacy?

Its latest lawsuit, the sixth, was aimed at the *Wall Street Journal*, the flagship newspaper of Dow Jones & Co. Liberty Lobby claimed that it was libeled, to the tune of $50 million in damages, by a 1984 column by Rich Jaroslovsky that suggested the organization was anti-Semitic and had some relationship with the American Nazi movement, and by a 1985 *Journal* editorial-page column by Suzanne Garment that discussed the Jaroslovsky column and Liberty Lobby's legal assault on the *Journal*.

The lawsuit was filed in November 1984. Then came more than a year of pre-trial legal maneuvering: primarily Liberty Lobby's demands for information about the preparation of the two columns it was attacking, and the *Journal*'s counter-demands for inside information about Liberty Lobby's publishing operations. A trial judge threw out the case in July 1986, finding that the charge of anti-Semitism was either a statement of opinion, or else was substantially true. The judge also concluded that there was no evidence whatsoever that anything the *Journal* had printed was published with "actual malice"—that is, with serious doubts about its truth.

It took more than another year for the case to go through the U.S. Circuit Court of Appeals, resulting in Judge Bork's ruling in the *Journal*'s favor. The Circuit Court, like the trial judge, found no "actual malice." Although Liberty Lobby lawyers had had more than a year to gather evidence to prove that the *Journal* had doubts about the truth of its story, no such evidence was produced, Bork concluded.

Essentially, Bork indicated, the issue had been settled when Liberty Lobby lost its case against Jack Anderson more than three years ago. And, recalling all of Liberty Lobby's libel claims, Judge Bork summed up: "This suit epitomizes one of the most troubling aspects of modern libel litigation: the use of the libel complaint as a weapon to harass." He suggested that many of Liberty Lobby's claims had suffered from "patent insufficiency," yet it had tied up Dow Jones & Co. "in over three years of costly and contentious litigation."

What Bork did not say, but what the press is free to say, is that the trouble traces back to the *Sullivan* ruling. By now, the press well knows that there are many defects in the *Sullivan* decision's supposed limitations on public-figure libel cases. But surely one of the decision's most glaring deficiencies is that it provides no mechanism for filtering out libel claims that are simply frivolous, with no hope of succeeding in court.

Merely by filing a lawsuit, a public figure is set loose on a long exploration of every detail of the gathering and preparation of the story or column that triggered the libel claim. The aim, of course, is to find evidence of the "state of mind" of the reporters and editors involved, to show reckless journalistic conduct ("actual malice," in legal terms). That can mean a veritable ransacking of a news organization's files, and hours and hours of pre-trial testimony by its staff.

Ironically, the Supreme Court has fashioned a way by which courts can quickly get rid of damage lawsuits that claim that some government official acted unlawfully in the line of duty, but it has not even considered doing so when the accusation of illegality is leveled against a news organization.

Liberty Lobby's three-year legal hounding of Dow Jones and the *Journal* was bad enough, given the outcome of that lawsuit. But what can be said about a system that allows such a pursuit to happen six times in a row? Lawyers and courts are inventive enough to find another way. It is time they do so—before the seventh suit is filed.

C H A P T E R   8

❦❦❦❦❦❦❦❦❦❦❦❦❦❦❦❦❦❦❦❦❦❦

Has the Story Been Ethically Researched and Presented?

- You are doing a television story on the plight of the homeless. As part of the piece, you dress up as a bag lady and take to the streets. Is it ethical to pass yourself off as someone you are not?

- As a reporter covering the city hall beat, your judgments often have a substantial impact on how government is perceived by your readers. The mayor has lately taken to meeting with you regularly to ask your advice on local issues. Is this an ethical relationship?

- Your job as fashion editor for a newspaper involves coverage of the lines available at a local department store. The store offers you an "employee discount" on merchandise. Can you ethically accept the discount?

Questions of ethics are nettlesome because written or unwritten codes cannot address all the issues a journalist will face. And "ethics" covers such a broad area that it is impossible to determine what, exactly, an ethical issue is. Many cases addressed in this book certainly fall into the realm of ethical dilemmas. The questions above, though, deal more with judgments relating to *professional conduct*, the primary focus of this chapter.

Discussion: Ethics in the Newsroom

Many ethical/professional-conduct decisions involve the three general areas illustrated above: misrepresentation, relationships with news sources, and favors given to reporters.

In general, decisions on misrepresentation center on the intent of the misrepresentation. Was it impossible to get the story any other way? In that case, the journalist is often given some latitude, but only after all the specifics have been evaluated on a case-by-case basis. For example, CBS "60 minutes" Executive Producer Don Hewitt has been quoted as attesting that "misrepresentation is probably not a good idea, but in specific cases it's a sensational idea."[1] Hewitt felt that the bag lady ruse (a real case to be examined in the following section) merited a degree of misrepresentation. The NBC and ABC television networks both officially frown on misrepresentation,[2] but also allow that in specific cases it is appropriate.

Source relationships are equally vexing. Most journalists would probably maintain that the "advice-giving" relationship with the mayor is unprofessional. Many reporters have confronted dilemmas related to attempts to co-opt them into an advice-giving role, with the implied result that they will give more favorable coverage to the official who is ostensibly acting on their ideas.

Decisions involving "freebies" are somewhat more clear-cut. News media have shown increasing reluctance to allow reporters to take freebies or otherwise receive special consideration from people or organizations that they cover. If we consider the issue objectively, many freebies border on being bribes. And if we examine the issue of bribes objectively, it seems apparent that there are many categories of bribery.

One such category is the job offer, an offer ostensibly related to the newsperson's skill. But according to Univerity of Kentucky journalism professor Bruce M. Swain, the job offer is sometimes an effort to get a troublesome reporter out of the news business and, in effect, buy the reporter's silence.[3]

1. Quoted in Palmer (1987), p. 20.

2. Attribution in Palmer (1987).

3. See discussion in Swain (1978), p. 18.

Clearly, it is wrong to take a bribe, but as is the case with most ethical issues, such as the above-mentioned job offer, the lines are not very distinct. An employee discount is obviously a bribe, but what about a free lunch? Posing as a bag lady seems relatively harmless—but is it correct for a reporter to pose as a police officer?

Applying Ethical Judgments to Journalistic Decisions

These judgments are a matter of degree, of course, and that is why precise limits are difficult to draw. Even the most experienced journalists don't have all the answers, nor do they speak with one voice on such issues. For example, when WNBC-TV (New York) anchor Pat Harper disguised herself as a bag lady, she was accused by some as exploiting the homeless via a journalistic misrepresentation.[4] But the consensus seemed to echo the belief that it was the best way to obtain the particular story— that is, a direct observation of what life is like for a homeless woman.

Practically speaking, it was the *only* way to get the story, a factor which bears on the reasoning process of a journalist confronted with a representation issue. Henry Schulte, professor of journalism at Syracuse University, faced such a situation as chief correspondent for United Press in Spain from 1956 to 1962. Under the dictatorship of Francisco Franco, the flow of information in Spain was severely limited, and Schulte faced a particular problem when events of international interest occurred.

"After a plane crash," Schulte said, "we would get calls immediately... questions from Ireland, say, or Belgium, on whether any nationals from their countries were on the plane. But when I called in my capacity as a reporter, all I would get would be, 'I'm sorry, I can't tell you that.' So I might call back and say, 'I'm a friend of Stanley Bzeierwicz, and I'm worried that he might have been on the flight that crashed.' And the response from the person on the other end of the phone might be, 'No.

---

4. See Palmer (1987).

The Decision-Making Process in Journalism

8.1   Henry Schulte, Professor, Newhouse School of Public
      Communications, Syracuse University. Photo by Christine
      Patsalos.

there were no foreigners on the plane.' "

Misrepresentation? In a way. Was it wrong? "I was working
in a dictatorship," Schulte said, "and my job was to get information. [Because of the circumstances] I might have gone about
it in a more devious way."[5]

Clearly, at least from the author's viewpoint, there was
nothing wrong at *gut-level* with Schulte's approach, nor with

5. Example provided by Schulte (1987).

Pat Harper's misrepresentation. Neither *feels* blatantly wrong or unethical. And while the gut-level test is far from infallible, it does have some commonsense application in other areas of ethics. For instance, what about releasing information classified by the government? Knowing that classified material often contains information which is not so much a state secret as a potential source of embarrassment to a bureaucrat, most reporters would probably not balk at breaking a classified story if the story dealt with government misuse of funds. But should a reporter disclose ship movements in wartime? No. Few would argue that case, including former CBS News president Fred Friendly, who, responding to that scenario, said: "I'm a citizen first, a reporter second."

A cup of coffee bought by an interviewee probably would be considered ethically compromising by few if any journalists. A free meal might. In fact, it is the policy of some (but not all) news organizations that a reporter always pays for his or her lunch. Accepting a free luxury cruise definitely would be a violation of ethics. In each case, the line is crossed when the issue grows from courtesy to bribery.

While those lines are indeed difficult to draw, many organizations have tried to draw them with varied success. Written codes of ethics are provided by several professional organizations including the Society of Professional Journalists, the American Society of Newspaper Editors; and the Radio-Television News Directors Association.[6] Local news organizations frequently have written codes of ethics as well. A 1985 survey published in the *Journal of Mass Media Ethics* showed that 59 percent of the news directors and editors responding had formal written statements of ethical policy.[7] Another study, published in *Journalism Quarterly*, indicated that three-fourths of responding newspaper managing editors said they had issued memos on ethical issues, and two-thirds said they had held seminars on the ethics.[8]

---

6. Listing taken from Davenport, L.D., and Izard, R.S. (1985–86).

7. From Davenport, L.D., and Izard, R.S. (1985–86).

8. Detailed by Anderson (1987).

Ethics have received growing attention in recent years, and some observers feel this is an outgrowth of the national agony of Watergate. Codes of ethics are a good first step for any journalist seeking to understand what is and what is not professional conduct.

What do those codes of ethics say? The content ranges widely, obviously, but there is some common ground. In many cases, the ethical codes deal with questions raised and discussed in other chapters. The following guidelines are reflective of a survey of written and unwritten codes dealing with professional conduct and take into account the gut-level judgment that comes from experience and common sense.[9]

Checklist: Is My Story Ethically Researched and Presented?

1. Did I at any time have an unprofessional relationship with the source of the story or parties involved in the story? You cannot be impartial, or at the very least *appear* impartial, if you have accepted gifts from an involved party, or acted as a consultant (paid or unpaid) or produced publicity material for that party. It is also important that you not hold a financial interest in areas which will be affected by your reporting. (This, of course, must be tempered with common sense; it would be very difficult to ascertain that someone who owns municipal bonds is in a conflict of interest if he or she writes about City Hall.)

2. Were representations made honestly and fairly during construction of the story? If you used anonymous sources, do you believe to the best of your judgment that the material you represent as fact is true? What about representations you made during research? In most cases, a certain amount of mis-

---

9. Codes include those of the *American Society of Newspaper Editors, Associated Press Managing Editors Association, Society of Professional Journalists, Chicago Sun-Times, Des Moines Register and Tribune, Washington Post,* and *Louisville Courier-Journal.* Codes reprinted in Swain (1978).

representation is considered forgivable if (a) it is the only way to get a story; (b) it harms no one; and (c) it is not an impossible contrivance. The bag lady case is one example. No one was harmed, and in actuality Pat Harper *could*, if she so chose, live on the streets and dress in old clothes. But posing as a police officer is never acceptable. It is a fundamental dishonesty and is an impossible contrivance which allows you privileges to which you could never be entitled as a private citizen.

3. Have I been objective? This is a tough call, but when stories involve close friends or cherished beliefs, it may be time to beg off. News executives generally respect the judgment of their reporters when those reporters remove themselves from a story because of lack of objectivity.

4. Have I been honest and truthful with the public and myself? The unattributed quote, for example, might read much more cleanly if it were rewritten the way you *wish* the source had said it. The unattributed anecdote might make the point more clearly if it were fictionalized. But avoid these practices because they are fundamental dishonesties.

Avoid the temptation to state as fact information which you have not checked for accuracy. If a piece of information comes from another source (a magazine article, for example) and you can't check it out yourself, attribute it to the magazine.[10] And, of course, never make a wholesale appropriation of someone else's material and pass it off as your own. That's known as plagiarism, and it is cause for dismissal at almost all news organizations.

Case History: The Philadelphia Inquirer *and the Three Unattributed Paragraphs*

Attribution is a thorny issue which cuts across a wide range of ethics and practices. In the case of the 1986 *Philadelphia Inquirer* article, questions about attribution first surfaced at a journalism panel discussion and became a national controversy. The dispute developed over several

---

10. Good standard advice echoed by author Paul Eddy in an *American Society of Newspaper Editors* panel discussion on anonymous attribution; Eddy quoted by Radolf (1987), p. 12.

paragraphs of unattributed description which were culled from an uncredited source, and which may have misled readers into believing those paragraphs were taken from the reporter's direct experience or interviews.

The following article, reprinted from *Editor & Publisher*, is a thoughtful analysis of a difficult ethical issue. The issue is especially troublesome because it is not clear-cut—there certainly was no blatant fraud on the part of the author of the *Inquirer* article—and it forces journalists to re-examine a technique they have all used *to some degree* during their careers.

Mountain or Molehill?
Six-month-old controversy over the lack of attribution in an award-winning newspaper article is still drawing opinions from editors

By Andrew Radolf

The lack of attribution involving about 200 words in an award-winning 5,000-word story in the *Philadelphia Inquirer* has touched off a controversy that has engulfed the newspaper industry from the Associated Press to the Pulitzer Prizes.

Although the controversy surfaced six months ago, it remains a much-discussed topic among certain newspaper editors who refuse to let the matter die.

At center stage in the debate is not only the story itself, but also John Perry, editor of the *Rome* (Ga.) *News-Tribune*, who has been accused of attempting to "cast a shadow" over a young journalist's first Pulitzer Prize with his contention that the missing attribution constituted "a possible breach of journalistic ethics."

Perry has also been accused of "irresponsible journalism" and with fanning the flames of the controversy to keep it alive. He has not only wound up feuding with AP over its refusal to electronic carbon the *News-Tribune*'s stories on the matter, but, after discovering an error in the *Inquirer*'s letter nominating Steve Twomey for the Pulitzer, has incurred the Philadelphia paper's wrath by questioning if the prize should be returned.

This is not the first time Perry has created a stir in the newspaper world. In 1985, he drew national attention with an *E&P* article that said newspapers did not have an obligation to be fair. He argued that newspapers were obligated to report with "accuracy, timeliness, incisiveness and pertinence," but said fairness

Courtesy *Editor & Publisher*.

"just" doesn't fit in with the other four. You cannot have all five [*E&P*, Dec. 28, 1985, p. 40]."

Perry also received newspaper industry attention when he was fired in 1983 as editor of the *Clearwater* (Fla.) *Sun* in a dispute with the publisher over the publisher's drinking a cup of coffee at a department head meeting in a conference room. Perry felt the publisher was violating his own ban on food and drink in carpeted areas and walked out of the meeting.

The *Inquirer* article that has raised the attribution questions, "America's Carriers: Ultimate Weapon or Easy Target," was published Oct. 5, 1986, in its *Sunday* magazine. Its author, Twomey, of the *Inquirer* staff, had spent time aboard the *USS America* in researching his article and mixed in vignettes of shipboard action with his discussion of the effectiveness and vulnerabilities of the U.S. supercarriers.

The article won a writing award from the American Society of Newspaper Editors and the 1987 Pulitzer Prize for feature writing.

The attribution question was first pointed out by Twomey himself at an early-bird session during the ASNE convention last April in San Francisco.

One of the two excerpts selected from Twomey's work for discussion consisted of three paragraphs about the sinking by an Exocet missile of the British frigate *HMS Sheffield* during the Falklands War. The paragraphs, which came at the last third of the article, were being used for a transition to discuss how vulnerable U.S. supercarriers were to these inexpensive but deadly missiles.

The paragraphs for discussion had been selected by Don Fry, associate director of the Poynter Institute for Media Studies, who was moderating the session.

Twomey pointed out first to Fry the night before, and then to those at the session, that the paragraph on the Exocet missile was not original work but paraphrasing based on his research, including passages about the *Sheffield*'s sinking in the book *The War in the Falklands*, co-authored by three British journalists who were members of the *Sunday Times* Insight Team.

"I don't think what I did was outside the norms of everyday practice," Twomey told *E&P*. He explained that the passage was "condensed" from information in the book and several other sources for the purpose of "getting in and getting out" of the sinking of the *Sheffield*.

"My purpose was not to give a blow-by-blow, minute-by-minute account," he said.

(Twomey is currently on leave from the *Inquirer* in order to be with his wife, who took a job at the *San Jose* [Calif.] *Mercury News,* another Knight-Ridder newspaper.)

Several editors present at the ASNE session asked Twomey if he had attributed the passage to the book, and became concerned that he had not. The lack of attribution, they felt, could result in readers being misled that information on the sinking of the *Sheffield* came from interviews Twomey himself had conducted.

One of those expressing concern was David Stolberg, assistant general editorial manager for Scripps Howard newspapers.

"I happen to be the one at the session who asked, 'Did you attribute it?' " Stolberg said. "My position has always been, when in doubt, attribute it. If that had been done, then all the flap would not have taken place.

"This is all the stuff [*Detroit Free Press* publisher] David Lawrence and the credibility study told us. We've got to be straight with the reader."

Stolberg suggested "an explanatory box someplace" could also have served the purpose of attribution if putting it in the text would have interrupted the story's flow.

While Stolberg took the position that attribution would have been better, he felt the lack of it was a minor journalistic infraction in an otherwise exemplary article.

"My feeling is, [the article] was deserving of the ASNE and Pulitzer prizes."

The questions raised at the session also prompted Anthony Day, editorial page editor of the *Los Angeles Times* and the person in charge of the ASNE awards program, to look into the matter. He eventually wrote to ASNE members what he characterized as "a long-winded letter about a tempest in a teapot."

Day continued, "Don [Fry] and I agreed that attribution would have been better, but it was no sin. It was, after all, a historical event. . . . It turns out that all accounts of the sinking of the *Sheffield* have basically the same source: a pool reporter."

Day also stressed that he, Fry and others who have examined Twomey's article all agreed that there is no question of plagiarism involved.

In a separate letter to the *News-Tribune,* Day said there was "never any question of Mr. Twomey's violating any common practice of journalistic ethics by failing to acknowledge the book from which he drew the description."

Gene Roberts, *Inquirer* president and executive editor, believes no attribution was necessary because Twomey was "dealing with something that's history, and doing it illustratively to make a point."

Roberts also remarked that accounts of the *Sheffield's* sinking came from a pool report put together by British Press Association reporter Peter Archer from his interviews with survivors.

"There was no reporter on board the *Sheffield*," Roberts said. "If Twomey attributed it to the book, the problem was the quote wasn't original to the book."

Roberts was referring to the quote, "My God, it's a missile," uttered simultaneously by two *Sheffield* officers. He said the quote appears without attribution in at least two books on the Falklands War, the other being *The Battle for the Falklands.*

Archer, according to Roberts, believes the quote came from his pool report and is in the public domain.

"The quote is exactly the same quote" in both books, Robert said, including the description of the officers speaking simultaneously. "That's why this is ridiculous."

Paul Eddy, one of *The War in the Falklands'* three co-authors, denied the passages relied on by Twomey came from pool reports.

"There are descriptions from pool reports, but what he lifted is not," Eddy told *E&P*. He said Twomey's paraphrasing was "based on" passages written from Insight Team interviews with the *Sheffield*'s captain in England and with the Exocet's French developer.

Eddy also said Twomey was "sloppy" in his paraphrasing. "The thing in the end that pissed me off is he got it wrong. He implies they evacuated the ship [right away] when they spent hours fighting the fire.

"I think as a general rule, if you're lifting stuff you haven't checked, it is helpful to let the reader know where it's come from. The assumption of the reader is that he's been around and happened to speak with people on the *Sheffield.*"

Twomey responded to Eddy's statements by pointing out the Exocet information in his article—such as the pounds of explosives in the warhead—is "a fact incredibly easy to obtain, like from *Jane's.*"

Twomey added that Eddy's contention that he got some information wrong makes attribution "even less of an issue. If I were

Eddy, I would be grateful I didn't attribute to him if I got it wrong."

The question of attribution in Twomey's story will be examined in an article for the *APME Bulletin* by Price Colman, managing editor of the *Stuart* (Fla.) *News.*

"No one's not recognized Twomey's writing ability and talents, but I feel it's a valid issue. The article's won two prizes. That makes it a seedling for the discussion," Colman said, adding that his piece focuses on the "larger question" of what the standards for attribution should be. "There's a lack of consensus."

Fry of the Poynter Institute also said that he wants to use the Twomey article as a springboard for an "industrywide discussion of larger attribution—passages et cetera—how to do it without interrupting the story's telling."

The Twomey matter probably would have remained an academic discussion over attribution had not John Perry also been at the early-bird ASNE session and decided to have his newspaper report on "an event he saw. I did not raise the issue."

After Twomey's story won the Pulitzer, Perry decided to assign Rebecca Masters to do a story on the attribution question. He wanted her to contact other editors for their views.

(The *Inquirer* has contended that Masters at first raised the issue of plagiarism with editors. This Masters denied. "We never brought up plagiarism at all. That's something someone else told them," she said. "We've looked at this as an issue of attribution.")

"My original point," Perry told *E&P,* "is not whether you attribute or don't attribute. In writing a colorful story, is it good journalistic practice to be so dramatic in your writing that you lead your reader to assume you were at the scene when you weren't?"

Masters' story, "Right to know who messengers are," appeared April 28 on the *News-Tribune*'s editorial page. It ran there, Perry said, because that was the only place the newspaper had space for it.

But in an italicized lead-in to Masters' story, Perry raised the question that the lack of attribution may be a "breach of journalistic ethics." While all of the other editors concerned about the lack of attribution have discussed it in terms of what constitutes "good journalistic practice," Perry was the only one to wonder about ethics.

Perry wanted the AP to pick up Masters' story, but the news service declined.

Perry ultimately sent a letter to AP president Louis D. Boccardi demanding to know the reasons why the news service had "killed" the story. Perry had previously sent the story and his chronology of events to the Georgia Associated Press News Council.

Perry also sent copies of Masters' story to other newspapers. One of those papers which decided to reprint it was the Denver *Rocky Mountain News.*

Perry pointed to the Denver paper's decision as proof that that [sic] other newspapers shared his concerns. He said AP should have picked up the story and let the editors make "their own decisions" about running it. He also wondered if the AP were "looking after a bigger client."

(At a later stage of the controversy, the Sunday *Atlanta Constitution and Journal* did its own story about the Twomey/Perry matter, and Perry renewed his feud with AP when the news service did not carry its own version of the story which he wanted to reprint in the *News-Tribune.)*

"We did not carry your story about the brief Twomey reference to the Falklands because, in our judgment, the accusation against him was picayune, if not groundless. . . I note without comment that the supposedly full package you sent me in your May 22 letter fails to include the letter to the editor of your own newspaper, from Anthony Day, disassociating himself completely from the shadow you are trying to cast on the Pulitzer award to Twomey."

Perry felt Boccardi's letter was a personal attack.

"All in God's world I was doing was reporting. I asked questions and, boy, did they not want that."

"That letter was written in response to a letter from John, that letter wasn't written to attack him," Boccardi said. "The letter stated my agreement with the news judgment that the AP had made. [The] ommission [sic] of that attribution in that circumstance did not justify casting a shadow on the award."

"Lou ought to be ashamed of himself. He's wrong," Perry responded to the allegation. "I'm trying to get a dialogue going. There is a dialogue going."

He added, "If AP had covered the thing, it would be over and done with."

However, Boccardi was not alone in believing that a shadow, however much undeserved, had indeed been cast over Twomey's prizes.

"I feel sorry for Twomey," Day said. "People are going to remember that Twomey got a prize and they are going to remember that there's something wrong with it."

Twomey declined to comment on whether he felt a shadow had been cast on his prize, or if Perry was being unfair. But he did ask why, if an industry discussion on attribution was what Perry wanted, his story was the only one being talked about.

The *News-Tribune*'s persistence in investigating Twomey's article resulted in phase two of the controversy: The newspaper discovered that the *Inquirer* had erred in its nominating letter to the Pulitzer board when it said Twomey had been aboard the *America* when it participated in the bombing of Libya.

Twomey was not. He had gone aboard a few weeks later.

Twomey recounted the night of the raid based on his interviews with the carrier's captain. In doing so, he relied on such new journalism devices as conveying the captain's thoughts and described the planes taking off for the raid in an active, you-are-there voice.

"My concern is not whether the reader thinks a reporter was there," Twomey commented. "My concern is to make the reader feel he was there."

The stylist approach led Perry to think otherwise; that Twomey had been aboard. In asking AP to check the matter out, Perry was informed by Boccardi—in the same letter he had seen as "attacking me"—about the error in the nominating letter.

That prompted another story by Masters, who in interviewing Roberts about the letter, asked if there had been "any discussion or thought in your mind as to whether the Pulitzer should be retained under the circumstances."

To which Roberts replied: "Are you out of your mind?"

Masters said she didn't think so; and Roberts said the *Inquirer* was "absolutely not" thinking of returning Twomey's Pulitzer.

Masters' story was headlined: "*Philadelphia Inquirer* keeps Pulitzer despite false info."

Perry defended the use of the word "false."

"False is something that's not true. I think that qualified. I think 'false' is the appropriate word," he said, although he also stressed that he was not accusing anyone of deliberately misleading the Pulitzer judges.

James Naughton, *Inquirer* deputy managing editor and the Pulitzer nominating letter's author, took full responsibility for the error.

"When I wrote that letter, I was going on the belief that Steve had been on the ship fortuitously," Naughton said. "I asked the foreign editor, and was told 'yes,' he had been on board. It was the wrong person to have asked. I should have asked the magazine editor."

Naughton also related that the *Inquirer*'s editors felt Twomey's description of the Libya raid was "clearly coming from the captain of the ship."

Perry said he was concerned that the error in the letter may have influenced the decision to award the Pulitzer Prize to Twomey.

"It's a logical question to ask. It wasn't accusatory," he said. "I would be surprised if a compelling nominating letter didn't have some impact."

Robert C. Christopher, secretary of the Pulitzer Prize board, said concern over the nominating letter itself is "kind of a fake issue. The prize isn't awarded on the basis of a covering letter. It didn't have any effect on the awarding of the prize."

The Pulitzer board was "aware of the situation," Christopher said, but felt no action was warranted. He remarked that "none" of them "felt confused" by Twomey's writing.

Christopher noted that when a nominating letter makes claims which may be germane, such as citing government action resulting from an investigation, the Pulitzer judges seek "independent confirmation."

Naughton and Roberts each, in separate conversations, accused Perry and the *News-Tribune* of "irresponsible journalism" in the way the newspaper pursued the story.

They pointed out, for example, that Perry assigned the first story to Masters, and she began asking questions before either one of them had read Twomey's story in its entirety. All they had had were the brief excerpts handed out at the ASNE convention.

"She asked questions that were not appropriate," Naughton said. "He [Perry] had a reporter calling people and asking about a story that the reporter and he had not even read. If he's looking for a learned journalistic discussion of attribution, that just doesn't seem to be what was occurring."

"I think [the controversy] developed because no one read the story," Roberts said. "As soon as people read the story, except for John Perry and a couple of others, there just hasn't been any concern about it. I do think it was irresponsible journalism."

Both Perry and Masters conceded that they hadn't read the story when they began looking into the matter.

"What I was following up on at the time was a controversy that erupted at the ASNE meeting. Everyone was looking at the same thing," Masters said, in explaining that only excerpts were available in San Francisco. Masters said she had tried to secure a copy of the story from the *Inquirer*, but was unable to get it from the library.

"The Pulitzer was just announced. They were inundated," she said.

Roberts himself finally sent Masters a copy, as did the Poynter Institute's Don Fry.

Perry said the *News-Tribune* did not publish its first story on the matter "until we had seen the article."

The *Inquirer*'s editors also questioned why Perry after so many months was still intent on pursuing the Twomey matter.

"I'm not sure what he's trying to accomplish," Naughton wondered.

Said Twomey, "I'm not going to question his motives, but I wonder why he continues. Perry's the only one who keeps it going."

Twomey was one of several people who pointed out that Perry has already succeeded in having the dialogue he's wanted, including having ASNE, APME, the Poynter Institute and the Pulitzer Prize board re-examine his story.

"I don't think he can say he didn't have his discussion," Twomey said. "There's been no information since the Pulitzers were announced. I just wish someone would say 'enough.' "

Perry has been described by former colleagues as everything ranging from "extremely idealistic" and "very talented" to "arbitrary" and "a fanatic."

"If it mattered to John Perry, he would pursue it vigorously. He would pursue it right or wrong," said one editor who worked under Perry at another newspaper.

"He would do just about anything to get publicity. John Perry loves the limelight," said another ex-colleague.

When they worked for Perry, he never expressed a great concern about attribution issues, they said. In fact, they all remarked that he had been a devotee of "interpretive journalism" and the belief, as one put it, that "if it's a fact, it's a fact. You don't have to attribute it. Wouldn't that [Twomey's *Sheffield* account] fall into the category of interpretive journalism?"

"I guess not to have stayed with it would have made me guilty of hit and run," Perry replied. "I didn't know in this business you were criticized for being consistent and sticking with it."

If the story involved the government, he would be "applauded" for his tenacity, Perry contended. "But this is a newspaper. You're not supposed to question them."

Where newspapers get their information remains a major journalistic and public concern, Perry explained of his continuing interest in the matter.

He pointed to the controversies that have derailed the campaign of Sen. Joseph Biden for the Democratic presidential nomination and threatened to do the same to that of Massachusetts Gov. Michael Dukakis, and to the flap over *Washington Post* reporter Bob Woodward's description in his book *Veil* of a hospital-room interview with [the] late CIA Director William Casey.

"All of that has to do with attribution and where information comes from," he said. "The subject is much hotter now than when we started. It validates our need to talk about this."

Segments of Twomey article that raised the attribution debate

Below are excerpts from Steve Twomey's ASNE and Pulitzer prize-winning article, "America's Carriers: Ultimate Weapon or Easy Target," which have generated controversy among newspaper editors.

It came out of the west just after lunch, skimming 10 feet above the South Atlantic at 680 miles per hour. On the bridge of the *Sheffield*, a British frigate, Lts. Peter Walpole and Brian Leyshon had seen a puff of smoke on the horizon but didn't know what it meant and hadn't seen the Argentine Super Etendard fighter. One mile out, they both recognized what was coming their way.

"My God," they said simultaneously, "it's a missile."

Four seconds later, the Exocet hit starboard amidships, above the water line, and veered down into the engine room, where its 363 pounds of high explosives detonated. In an instant, *Sheffield* lost electrical power and communications. Fires broke out. The edge of the hole in the ship's side glowed red from the blazes, but there was no water pressure to put them out. As flames crept toward the magazine, where ammunition is stored, the crew abandoned the *Sheffield*.

* * *

Libya. They were actually going to hit Libya. Night had fallen. It was April 14, 1986. Allen looked down from the bridge at a dimly lighted flight deck jammed with aircraft, bombs and bullets bound for Benghazi. It was no drill. "I don't believe we're really doing this," he thought. "It's just unbelievable."

The crew had manned battle stations in record time. "All you have to do is tell somebody, 'We're going to go kill something,' and the level of interest goes up logarithmically. I mean people become—they're motivated."

Thirty-eight planes from America would go. Somewhere in the

The Decision-Making Process in Journalism

darkness of the Mediterranean, the scene was being repeated on the Coral Sea. One by one, planes roared away. The most beautiful were the F-14s because, in order to get extra lift, they always flipped on their afterburners just before the "cat stroke," sending twin cones of flames 20 feet down the flight deck and lighting up the dark area.

CHAPTER 9

Is It Worth the Consequences?

- During a morning newscast, you run a story about the brutal murder of a city native. A young man was literally dismembered in a bathtub, and—taking facts from the police reports—you describe the crime in detail. Later that morning, you receive a call from the father of the youth, who begs you not to run the story because it is so disturbing to the dead youth's family and friends.

    Do you kill the story?

- A woman witnesses a bank robbery and gets a close look at one of the robbers. You have the woman's name in your story. She calls and asks you not to use her name because she is afraid of reprisals from the criminal.

    Do you take her name out of the copy?

- You have solid evidence that a judge is carrying on an affair with a woman known to have criminal connections. Running the story will ruin the judge. You decide that the story will run . . . and the judge kills himself.

    Did you do the right thing?

Journalism can be a glamorous and exciting business, but it can also be a tough business. The decisions you make can have a major impact on people's lives.

Discussion: Balancing the Story and the Consequences

The death of his son was a horrifying blow to the man who called a news department to beg the reporter not to run the murder story. The reporter who took the call[1] knew that there was no way the story could be killed. It was a major event, and soon it would be picked up by other television and radio stations in the community, along with the evening paper. Killing the story on one station would be both unprofessional and pointless.

But was it simply the reporting of the murder that upset the father so? Possibly not; it appeared, after some questioning, that the graphic details of the murder were the most mortifying factor to the victim's family. After some reflection—reflection which included the fact that this story dealt with *people* and not just *news*—it became apparent that the story could be reported without much of the lurid detail of the early newscasts. That compromise did seem to help the family.

What about the woman who witnessed the bank robbery? A panel of news directors considering that hypothetical question agreed that there is no compelling reason to use the name of the witness. Using the name would not advance the story in any way and probably would endanger the woman. In short, the story was just as good with or without the name.

The suicide of the judge is not a hypothetical case.[2] It occurred after a series of articles co-authored by former *Denver Post* reporter Jay Whearley. Whearley, now executive editor of *Worcester Magazine* in Massachusetts, has regrets about the outcome but believes that running the story was the right thing to do.

How Decisions Are Made

When Whearley was investigating the story of corruption in a small Colorado town called Trinidad, he originally opposed the

---

1. Experience of author as anchor/reporter, WENY Television, Elmira, NY, 1976.

2. Account from interview with Whearley (1987).

idea of running the story about the judge's affair. He was persuaded that the story had merit during conversations with his partner and city editor.

What eventually convinced Whearley that it was right to write a story that would ruin the judge's career? The line was crossed when it became clear that the affair could compromise the judge's responsibilities to the public. "One of his girlfriends ran a brothel," Whearley said. "Prostitutes from this brothel could appear before the judge. Therefore, his decisions were tainted."

The judge hanged himself shortly after the story appeared. Whearley recalls "being very sad when that happened . . . but the Trinidad story helped people, too. It made them aware of a system where corruption had become the norm."

"In the back of every editor's mind," Whearley explained, "there's a hypothetical person who is reasonably intelligent— no genius, but smart enough—and is concerned with the good of society. That imaginary person is like a weathervane. Does that imaginary person feel the story is worth the consequences? If so, pursue it."

While there is a popular conception that journalists run stories regardless of the possible consequences, that is simply not the case. When someone can be hurt, judgments are weighed at every step: Does that imaginary intelligent reader, viewer, or listener *need* this information? Does the public's need to know outweigh the consequences to the affected parties?

Clearly, people who have placed themselves in compromising situations have a very weak case when pleading that a story be killed. NYU's Richard Petrow maintains: "The people who call up and say, 'Don't use the story of my shoplifting arrest. It'll kill my grandmother' . . . well, they should have thought of that before they stole something." WJAR-TV (Providence, Rhode Island) news director John Baer concurs: "Calls from affected parties have no bearing on journalistic decisions."

But when people are drawn into a situation, consideration must be given to the consequences versus the public good. The *Detroit Free Press* faced such a dilemma in the case of the politician who attended a campaign rally shortly after his son had committed suicide. The decision? Don't run the story.[3] The managing editor at the time, Stephen Seplow, according to *The Washington Journalism Review*, originally felt that it was not right to run the story because "people deal with their grief in different ways [and perhaps going to the rally was the politician's way of dealing with his grief]." Now, however, Seplow thinks the decision was wrong. The story should have run because it showed "a guy out of touch with reality."[4]

Decisions on whether or not to publish material often center around private lives of public officials. Witness the ongoing and seemingly endless attention paid to the Gary Hart story during the presidential primaries in 1988. That incident reinforced what has become the rule: Editors in almost all cases echo the prevailing sentiment that private details should be published when they affect the individual's performance in public office.

Criteria for Evaluating Worth versus Consequences

The following questions may help you sort through some of the more difficult questions faced by a journalist. If you are in doubt about whether a story or a fact in a story is worth the possible consequences, ask the following questions:

1. Did the affected party bring the situation on himself or herself? If so, that person is responsible for the consequences of the story.

2. Is there a compelling reason for the public to know? There is no justification for publicizing embarrassing details of a private person's life just for the sake of publishing a lurid story. But if that person in some way consents to being in the public eye or is thrust into the limelight (see the guidelines on *Privacy* in chapter 7), then the consequences may be warranted by the newsworthiness of the story. If the person in question is a public

---

3. Detailed by Stepp (1986).
4. See Stepp (1986), p. 39.

official, and the details may affect his or her public performance, there is usually ample justification for running the story.

3. Is someone likely to be hurt by accident? Syracuse University's Henry Schulte points out that there may be times when you have to hurt someone intentionally, but you must never hurt someone by accident. Carefully evaluate all the facts and quotes in a controversial story. Be sure they do not damage someone who does not deserve to be tarred with the same brush used on the main subject.

4. Will the mechanics of the media hurt someone unnecessarily? Syndicated columnist Ellen Goodman notes that someone saying "no comment" on television appears much more the villain than someone who refused comment in print.[5] Is it really necessary to use the televised "no comment"? Could you be making an innocent person look guilty?

That decision, along with most of the decisions discussed in this book, is a choice typical of many of the judgments made by a working journalist. It's a decision made half in the head and half in the heart—and a decision made best by the journalist who can effectively balance the rights of individuals with the public's need to know.

Case History: Covering the Worcester Fire Department

Worcester, Massachusetts, is the second largest city in New England and faces the usual big-city problems. *Worcester Magazine* writer Matthew Maranz was assigned to look into one of those problems: the difficulties faced by the city's fire department. Maranz documented cases which purported that the fire department had suffered from insufficient manpower and equipment.

It was a good story, but it was almost Maranz's last story. After the work appeared, Worcester's fire chief announced his retirement, ostensibly for health reasons. But *Worcester Magazine* editor Jay Whearley stated that contacts in the fire department suggested that Maranz's story precipitated the retirement.

---

5. Quoted by CBS News correspondent Mike Wallace and G.P. Gates (1984), p. 423.

Had this young reporter ruined the career of a public servant? "I was kind of numb when I heard about the [chief's] retirement," Maranz recalled. "In fact, I felt terrible. I wasn't prepared for it. You hear a lot about the power of the press, but nowhere do you hear about the human interest, what the stakes are."

Maranz was ready to quit the business, but he was convinced that he should continue as a reporter by private conversations with his editor and—in an unusual move, to be sure—by an editorial which ran in a following edition of the magazine.

Presented here is the story that reportedly led to the chief's resignation, followed by the editorial response. Some important points to consider when you try to evaluate whether the story in question was worth the consequences are:

1. Note that Maranz "followed the book" when he wrote the story. Ample opportunity was provided for comment and rebuttal (see the discussion on fairness in chapter 4), although that opportunity was not taken.

2. Consider the fact that editor Whearley is not a newcomer to dealing with unfortunate consequences. Note how he brought his experience as a reporter with *The Denver Post* into play.

3. A point for discussion: As readers, we have no way of verifying the facts of the story, but there does seem to be a reasonable case made that lives could be at stake because of conditions within the fire department. Does this, in your opinion, override the possible negative consequences or embarrassment suffered by city officials?

Worcester's Fire Department

· *How safe is the public?*
· *How safe are the firemen?*

Matthew Maranz

Constance Walker probably never gave much thought to such issues as the Worcester Fire Department's response time to emergencies, the quality of the department's fire-fighting equipment, or whether it takes three-, four-, or five-man crews on each fire truck to adequately protect Worcester residents. But when such issues are discussed officially and unofficially today in Worcester, her name often comes up.

Courtesy *Worcester Magazine*.

Is It Worth the Consequences?

The 35-year-old woman was trapped on the fifth floor of a building on Main Street that caught fire on Aug. 9, 1985. She managed to make her way to a window and probably saw Worcester fire crews arrive at the scene and attempt to get to her. But already suffering second and third-degree burns, Walker could wait no longer and either fell or jumped from the inferno and to her death.

At that exact instant, the fireman and ladder that could have saved her life were between the third and fourth floors. "We missed her by 15 seconds—tops," an exasperated Capt. Michael L. McNamee told *Worcester Magazine* in a recent interview. His frustrated tone suggested that the victim's life could have been spared.

Had the Worcester Fire Department done everything it was capable of doing or that could be reasonably expected at the time, then regardless of whether firefighters missed saving Walker's life by 15 seconds or 15 minutes wouldn't have made any difference— her death probably would have been regarded as an unavoidable tragedy. But there are knowledgeable authorities on fire safety who argue that the death of Constance Walker, while certainly a tragedy, just as certainly could have been avoided.

McNamee, for instance, insists that crucial time and quite possibly the opportunity to save her life were lost because the first truck to arrive did not have enough manpower to lift the 45-foot, 400-pound ladder. McNamee—a 15-year WFD veteran who works in the department's training division, a member of the WFD Firefighters' Union Safety Committee and a highly regarded crusader on behalf of bettering the local department—notes that while the raging flames drew closer to Walker, pushing her farther out the window, firemen 50 feet below scrambled to find a *civilian* to help them raise the ladder.

"If there were enough men on the truck, the ladder would have gone up faster, and she quite probably would have been plucked through the window," McNamee recalls as he shakes his head.

Considering woeful official neglect, an undermanned work force, outdated equipment and a festering morale problem, New England's second-largest fire department along with the residents of Worcester have been "unbelievably lucky" when it comes to fire safety, says Fire Lt. Phil Sullivan, also a member of the Union Safety Committee. About the city administration, Sullivan says, "They have the hugest rabbit's foot I've ever seen. They've been courting disaster for years and they've gotten away with it.

The Decision-Making Process in Journalism

That's a miracle...that's just sheer dumb luck."

As the Walker case points out, however, Worcester hasn't been consistently lucky and there are many more "horror stories" to tell, according to McNamee.

Consider:

- An elderly man died in a 1978 blaze on Richard St. at which the fire department's initial response was to send two trucks with a combined total of five men. Two firefighters, who went into the building without air masks rather than lose precious time taking the equipment out of suitcases, could not get to the victim through all the smoke.

- A five-alarm disaster at 728 Main St. on July 11, 1973, in which 10 people were killed. On that particular night, McNamee recalls, "There wasn't a company in the city that had four men on it." (Five firefighters per company is the generally recommended figure for effective manpower.)

Sullivan and McNamee openly discuss the WFD and its problems because, as Sullivan puts it, "We are already so deeply involved it doesn't matter if we use our names." But very few others within the department are willing to say anything publicly about the safety issues confronting both the department and city.

"Please understand our situation," says a station captain who agreed to talk with a reporter only after he was promised that his name wouldn't appear in print. "We all have our bosses, and they have instructed us to watch what we say. We can't say anything that is embarrassing to the city."

Chapter 12, Section 9 of the Worcester Fire Department Rules and Regulations states, "All members of the department shall refrain from adverse public criticism concerning the actions of any superior and they shall not publicly express disapproval of the policies and practices of the department. Constructive recommendations may be made through the channels of communication."

Several firefighters expressed concern over job reprisals if they talked with the news media although, as one fireman put it, "A lot of firefighters have probably wished the *Worcester Magazine* did a story on us."

"You want us to talk about the department?" asked another fireman who requested anonymity. "The best place to talk is in some bar after our shift is over. And it will take years to talk about it," he added with a smile. So *WM* did go to bars, coffee shops, homes and practically every possible site imaginable for the clandestine interviews. But one need go no further than the source of much of the firemen's concern and anger, Chief James F. Nally, to understand the basis of the problems within the WFD.

In his 1982 annual report to the city administration and to the city council, Nally said there were three critical criteria for an effective fire department; adequate manning, proper equipment and effective leadership.

But little, if anything, has changed since that report was turned in. And as Councilor Raymond Mariano notes, "In terms of those three areas there are critical questions about the type and age of our equipment, there is a shortage of men—so one man is doing the job of two men, sometimes three—and the leadership is being questioned from within the department.

"The fire department is not providing the type of fire protection we could, or should have," Mariano continues. "They [firefighters] are doing an outstanding job given the shortage of manpower and a host of other safety issues, but public safety is not at the level I'd like to see."

In simpler terms, the councilor says, "We're in big trouble." A primary reason for Mariano's gloomy assessment—and a point worth keeping in mind when considering complaints about the WFD—is that the department more often than not sends out companies with three and four men on emergency calls.

When Local 1009—Worcester's chapter of the International Association of Firefighters—surveyed its membership for their primary safety concerns in February 1987, 95 percent of those responding listed the manning issue as one of the department's two top priorities, according to McNamee. And the union isn't alone in its concern: Both Nally and City Manager William J. Mulford have labeled manpower as a key problem within the WFD.

"There are tons of problems" in the department, says WFD District Chief Jack Fenton, who is president of the union, "but they have all boiled down to manning."

Mulford declined to discuss the WFD manning issue because it is among items currently under discussion in labor contract talks between the city and the department. He did say there was some confusion as to whether manning was a politically negotiable issue in the contract talks, then added that he did not wish to discuss any aspect of the fire department until an agreement was reached.

A 1986 report on WFD manpower prepared by Nally and

submitted to the city administration summarizes the problem. "The number of personnel (468). . . has made the maintenance of an acceptable level of fire protection very questionable."

According to a widely cited study conducted by the Dallas (Texas) Fire Department, "A direct correlation exists between staffing levels and performance quality." The research, first conducted in 1969 then updated in 1983, notes that, "Manpower obviously plays a role in terms of the ability to coordinate the functions that must occur simultaneously. When you decrease the number of firefighters but not the number of tasks to be performed, you increase the number of tasks each firefighter must perform, or combine the firefighters you have to complete each task, which in turn delays the operation."

An Insurance Services Office report for Worcester recommends "at least five members, including an officer, be on duty at all times with each engine and ladder company." And Chief Nally himself responded to a federal survey of fire department crew sizes and called a crew with fewer than five members "undermanned."

Of the 28 comparably sized cities used for the ISO survey, only nine—including Worcester—allow undermanned companies to respond to emergencies. Cities such as Hartford, Bridgeport and New Haven, Ct., never allow undermanned companies on the street.

In the minds of many authoritative sources, the only possible outcome of inadequate manning is the decline of the WFD's capacity to protect the public.

"The results are inescapable," concludes a report issued by the Worcester Firefighters' Union Safety Committee: "There will be greater property loss, an increase in the number and probably the severity of injuries, and a greater probability of deaths occurring in our city."

The Dallas study concluded that a six-person crew is optimum for the safety of both the public and firemen themselves. A five-person crew is called 80 percent as effective as a six-person crew; a four-person crew only 52 percent as effective as a six-person crew. But a three-person crew—which the study blames for significant overtaxing of the force and increased fire damage—is considered only 32 percent as effective as the optimum.

During the day shift on Saturday, July 12, 17 of the 24 WFD engine and ladder companies ran with only three-person crews. Monitoring WFD staffing, *WM* determined that 216 of the 335 crews on duty that week consisted of only three men each.

Excluding the Rescue Squad, only one company ran with five men during the following week.

This severe undermanning that hinders performance quality apparently is made more dramatic by the high number of firemen using summer vacations. However, a WFD source emphatically states that manning shortages within the department are not a seasonal phenomenon. Each shift averages 13 three-man crews, the source told *WM*.

From Jan. 1, 1985, to Feb. 28, 1987—a 26-month period that includes 29,206 tours of duty—59 percent of the WFD's engine and ladder companies ran with only three men, according to the Union Safety Committee. Two percent (572) of the tours ran with only two men—a crew size labeled "useless" by a WFD station captain and a number not even considered in any of the studies obtained by the union. (Worcester City Council has since passed an ordinance prohibiting two-man companies.) In addition, 16 percent of the companies had no direct supervision by an officer.

Sullivan, who believes four men can do a decent job fighting fires, says "three-man crews can do the job, but not do it well." Combining the textbook response of the training division with the reality of fighting a fire in Worcester with inadequate manning, Sullivan describes what firefighters encountered on many of the more than 10,000 calls they responded to in a fiscal 1985-86:

"Say the first company in only has three guys. The first thing you do when you see fire is drop a guy at the hydrant. That guy is lost. He can't leave the hydrant until he sends water. The driver is at the pump, the hydrant man is at the hydrant and whoever is the last guy left in the three-man company has to go in by himself and effect a rescue by himself. . . you know one guy can only do so much."

One firefighter could not do it all by himself in an April 25, 1983, blaze at 79 Mill St. Wearing 60 to 70 pounds of protective equipment, the firefighter battled dense smoke and flames to save a woman's life. Tragically, there were two women in the building at the time.

"By the time he got her down three flights of stairs and went back in for No. 2, it was too late," McNamee explains. "The fire had come right across the third floor. Had he had a partner. . . there's a good probability that they would have grabbed her."

Operating at one-third of the optimum level of effectiveness on nearly 60 percent of all tours over the past two years has put both firefighters and citizens at increasing levels of risk. Undermanned crews hinder the department's initial response and, according to a basic tenet of fire-fighting, "What happens in the first five minutes of a fire determines what happens during the next three hours." The more time required to perform the critical functions—removal of occupants, containment of the fire, then extinguishing it—the less likely a victim will survive. *The National Fire Protection Association Handbook* also blames poor response time for small fires that expand into large-loss fires.

Without enough manpower to contain the fire, firefighters say any fire almost automatically turns into a multiple-alarm incident, just to get more men at the scene. Firefighters told *WM* that the additional equipment usually isn't necessary to battle two-or-more-alarm fires and the trucks usually sit idle. Besides increasing the department's cost per fire, the automatic second alarm robs other parts of the city of potentially needed men and equipment.

"If you have every company at one fire, and you get a fire somewhere else, someone is going to lose their life," one WFD source says.

Inadequate manning also subjects firefighters to greater risk. Forced to execute tasks designed for more than one person, one firefighter in a three-man crew must pull a 300-pound hose. In training school, that same firefighter accomplished the task with assistance from at least two other firemen. In addition, the smaller crews pose a threat to individual firefighters because it becomes impossible for each member to keep track of coworkers. "Fire rescue is like swimming—you don't go in alone," McNamee says. "We fall through a floor and we're alone, nobody knows it. They find us after the fire."

In a 1986 report, Chief Nally blamed the restraints of Proposition 2½—the 1980 referendum limiting a municipality's expenditures by capping real estate taxes—for the manpower shortage. He called for the department to be strengthened to pre-Prop. 2½ levels.

However, available statistics show the manning crisis long precedes Prop. 2½. A 1973 report by the Insurance Services Office found the 95 firefighters, the average number of on-duty crew members per shift, to be inadequate. City Councilor Jordan Levy told a newspaper reporter in 1978 that the fire department "was operating a vitally important department with severe understaffing." Mariano argues that Proposition 2½ is "a great excuse that is a little weak."

Instead, Mariano and the firefighters' union cite years of poor planning as the source of the manning crisis. When firefighters left the force in the past, the city did not allocate money to fill the vacancies—establishing a pattern of dwindling numbers of firefighters.

The long-term solution is hiring additional firefighters. Fenton says the union "would be happy with four men" on each company and requested 75 new hirings, enough to ensure that all crews had three privates and an officer. Chief Nally recently recommended hiring 45 new firefighters. City Manager Mulford has allocated funds for 21 new firefighters and asked for $283,663 in supplementary funds to add another 24.

The 1985-86 WFD budget was $13 million and hiring enough firemen to guarantee four firefighters on each crew would require an additional $1 million per year. But additional hirings, even if done immediately, would not solve the problem right away. Any firefighters the department recruited today would not become members of the force until December because of background checks and training, according to McNamee.

As if the manning issue weren't enough to fuel a growing morale problem within the WFD, many city firefighters are forced to work out of stations that some argue are candidates for condemnation. After a tour of the city's fire stations, Mariano reported, "We are jeopardizing the safety of the firefighters because of the building problems. The conditions are deplorable. We are not even doing the things [enforcing building codes] we require of everybody else."

Four stations—Cambridge St., Webster Sq., Quinsigamond Village and Brown Sq.—are considered by firefighters to be the most hazardous. All four were designed for horse-drawn fire apparatus and were built in the 19th century. Because conditions such as those found during visits to the city's fire stations can occur only after decades of neglect, it is hard to understand how the blame can be placed on a referendum enacted only seven years ago.

The prevailing attitude within the WFD is, a source says, "If it ain't broke, don't fix it." Some money may well have been saved by skipping routine maintenance, but the result is that in 1987, many fire stations are definitely broke. Estimates run beyond $1 million to repair just the four previously mentioned stations.

Firefighters refer to the Cambridge St. Station (Engine Company No. 14) as "The Fountains" because during a heavy rain, the plumbing system backs up and as much as a foot of raw sewage floods the cellar. Overflowing toilets depositing feces on the station's floor cause obvious sanitary problems and forced firemen to evacuate the station this past spring. For two night shifts, Engine Company No. 14 was forced to work out of the Southbridge St. Station, increasing response time. Other problems at Cambridge St. include a communications system that often is difficult to understand. Response time obviously can be slowed if a crew can't understand where it is to respond.

Then there is the order from Chief Nally prohibiting parking on the canal side of the Webster Sq. Station—issued last month because slate was falling off the station's roof and damaging cars parked in the lot. Some of the slate falls from the station's tower where a tree mysteriously grows inside each spring. "It's our pride and joy," a firefighter says caustically.

Quinsigamond Village Station also contends with descending wall and ceiling fragments. A plastic covering hangs beneath the decaying ceiling to protect firefighters from falling plaster, but some crew members have been injured by falling debris. In addition, rain pours through the station's walls, some of the floor boards are missing and other areas of the floor have rotted away. A leaking roof, coupled with a drain that freezes in the winter, has sculpted a hole about a foot in circumference in the first-floor tapper's room.

Says one fire commander: "These buildings would be condemned if they were privately owned." It should be noted, however, that Worcester Code Commissioner Carl H. Koontz recently told the city's Public Safety Committee that "some corrective work needs to be done . . . but there are no safety problems with the stations." Koontz has $27,000 in his budget for ordinary maintenance and believes descriptions of the four stations are "somewhat exaggerated."

Deterioration due to aging also affects the department's fire trucks. According to the *National Fire Protection Association Handbook*, a first-line pumper should remain on duty for 10-15 years. But only three of Worcester's 16 pumpers were purchased within the past decade—leaving 81 percent of the city's pumpers out of compliance with the NFPA standards. Three pumpers—Engine 16 (1965), Engine 3 (1967), and Engine 12 (1967)—have more than 20 years' service and two more are in their 19th year. During fiscal 1985-86, pumpers purchased in the 1960s (carrying 1960's fire-fighting equipment) made 4,797 runs—3,060 more than pumpers purchased in the 1980s.

Is It Worth the Consequences?

The department also has fallen behind its timetable for replacing aging apparatus. Three pumpers and two ladder trucks that were scheduled to be relegated to spare status during the past two years remain on active duty.

"By definition," a WFD source says, "we have good equipment . . . but it's in a poor state of repair. It's far below top running condition."

The manning situation, facilities and equipment have all taken their toll on the firefighters' morale—a situation worsened by the failure of their union and the city to agree on a new labor contract. A pact the union bargaining committee accepted was overwhelmingly defeated by the members and those bargaining on behalf of the firemen argue that the city has asked for too many concessions.

But the firefighters' discontent also stems from "fire-fighting professionals not being treated professionally," as one source puts it. The solution, they argue, appears to be in finding a leader who will be an advocate for the department, a leader who will not accept continued neglect and a leader who will challenge the city for more men and better equipment. They argue that Chief Nally is not such a man.

Several WFD officers point out that after acknowledging the shortage of manpower, delays in the apparatus replacement program and the seriously deteriorating conditions of the fire stations, Nally's 1986 report concludes, "The department has managed to provide an acceptable level of fire protection for the citizens of the city." He also thanked the "city family" for providing the equipment and additional manpower.

"The crux of the problem is that the chief won't fight for us," says a WFD captain. He cites as an example this year's St. Patrick's Day Parade incident in which Nally prohibited the firefighters from marching with their union flag. The firefighters responded by exchanging their dress uniforms for street clothes and marching with their flag as an independent group. Firefighters say that more members of the force marched in that parade than in any of recent memory.

"The chief," another source says, "was an excellent street chief and a good tactician, but he is a lousy administrator . . . We feel the chief doesn't care about us . . . there may be five men in this whole department supporting the chief."

"The union is doing the fire chief's job right now," says one high-ranking WFD official. "The chief of the department right now . . .

should be talking to you. Not us. A good chief would be up there sticking up for his men."

City Council apparently agrees.

"It seems that whenever there is a cause for concern, the firefighters have to initiate the action themselves," Councilor Joseph M. Tinsley said during an April City Council meeting. "Where has the administrative body of the Fire Department been? We have never seen these issues raised by the administration."

"Why weren't these issues raised by Nally or Mulford?" Councilor Sara J. Robertson asked at the same meeting.

More than a dozen phone calls and in-person attempts to contact Nally were made by *WM* but each time he declined to be interviewed on or off the record. According to his spokeswoman, Theresa Wayman, Nally did not want to discuss any controversial issues or respond to any of the comments made about him.

In the course of its research and well after Nally was aware of this magazine's interest in the WFD, *WM* obtained a copy of a memo circulated July 24 instructing firefighters not to talk to the media about "fire operations" without approval from the fire chief or a commanding officer. Several commanding officers, incidentally, told *WM* that they had been verbally instructed not to discuss internal problems of the department.

"The only reason the job is getting done out there," says one WFD officer, "is because, when the fan turns brown, the guys dig deep. The guys have a lot of personal pride and they do respond . . . but it takes a lot out of us."

Although he admits public recognition of the problems faced by WFD, firefighters can only help their side in the current contract talks, Union President Fenton adamantly denies firefighters are talking about negotiable issues or searching for a bargaining advantage.

"This has nothing to do with contracts," he says. "This is about safety."

Some advice for a rookie reporter
Column written by Editor Jay Whearley

Until last week, those of us who work with Matthew Maranz at *Worcester Magazine* talked more about his potential than what he'd actually done as a journalist. First as a *WM* intern—assigned here from Clark University—then as an editorial assistant, and finally as a writer for the magazine, Maranz had demonstrated considerable skill both with words and with people. Even though I tried to make sure his editorial progress here was gradual, he continually pushed for more and better story assignments. Several weeks ago, when he turned in the On the Road column that appeared in last week's issue, it was obvious Matt Maranz couldn't be held back any longer. The column, about the changing character of a neighborhood bar, was as compassionate and as well-written as anything that has appeared in this publication or any other in the area for quite some time.

It was about that time that yet another plea came into this office to put together a story about the Worcester Fire Department. There had been numerous other requests for *WM* to look into the situation, but all demanded anonymity as a condition for talking to us. I hesitated to go along with such a step because stories based on anonymous sources simply aren't as credible with readers. Maranz and another writer were assigned to look into the story and he was out the door in minutes. The other staffer had a few stories to clean up before she could join in the investigation, but it didn't make any difference. Three days later Maranz had the situation well in hand. He went from fire station to fire station seeking answers to questions about the safety of both the public and the firefighters themselves.

Before long the pieces of the puzzle started fitting together for Maranz. Apparently because of official neglect more than any other factor, the WFD was losing effectiveness. Maranz was able to document cases of WFD crews arriving at fire scenes without the manpower to rescue those in danger. In one case, a woman was trapped in a burning building as firemen five stories below tried to enlist a civilian to help them with a 45-foot, 400-pound ladder. The woman later fell or jumped to her death.

At the heart of all the internal complaints, Maranz found, were accusations that the WFD was undermanned by 75 firefighters, that a good portion of the WFD's fire-fighting equipment was out of date, and that there was little support from the top levels of the WFD and the City Administration.

City Manager William J. Mulford declined to respond to *WM* questions about these and other complaints, noting that the city currently was involved in contract negotiations with the firefighters. Maranz tried a dozen times, personally and by telephone, to gain comment from Fire Chief James Nally. Each time, the chief declined.

The Decision-Making Process in Journalism

Maranz' story appeared in last week's (July 29) issue of *Worcester Magazine* and, all in all, was an admirable effort by a young reporter. First cover stories or Page 1 bylines in this business are as memorable as first girlfriends, and as hard as the 21-year-old reporter tried to disguise it, he was proud of his effort.

At least he was until the following day when he learned Chief Nally had taken an early retirement from his job. Merely months into a promising career, Maranz appeared ready to chuck it all. Although the City Administration and other news media in town took pains to suggest that the chief's decision to leave was based solely on health considerations and was made the day before the story appeared, WFD contacts suggested the *WM* article was the proverbial last straw for Nally.

Maranz was sickened that his story might have been a factor in the chief's decision to leave. In the course of Maranz' research, he was told often that Nally had the admiration and respect of other firemen when he was working on the street. Unhappiness within the ranks occurred after Nally was named chief—and given the circumstances, there's some doubt that anyone could have satisfactorily dealt with both the men on the street and the City.

Deeply troubled, Maranz questioned me about the power of the media and the considerable potential for the abuse of that power, the lack of cut-and-dried guidelines for dealing with such situations and the callousness some in the business have when they encounter them. I tried to be of some help, but I know I wasn't. Eleven years ago, you see, a county court judge in southeastern Colorado committed suicide following a series of stories written by another reporter and myself. I asked myself those same questions at the time and continue to do so to this day.

And maybe that's not such a bad thing after all.

Courtesy *Worcester Magazine.*

AFTERWORD

After all the arguments have been put forth and all the sources listed, there is a temptation to propose a glib summary—a blanket theory which purportedly explains all the facets considered in the work.

Some constructive thought, though, makes it obvious that reading this book is only the beginning of the process of developing and understanding news judgment. This book began with the premise that there are no easy answers, and it must end on that same assumption.

However, close examination of the case studies put forth in *The Decision-Making Process in Journalism* reveals two common threads which—while certainly not "formulae" for news judgment—seem to run through most cases.

First, our exploration of journalists and their decisions shows that good news judgment is the type of judgment that would be made by any mature man or woman who is reasonably intelligent (though not an expert on every subject) and compassionate. Sitting judges in courts of law often apply the standard of "what a prudent man or woman would do" in a particular circumstance. A journalist can and should follow the same course. When in doubt, start your thinking process not by dwelling on journalistic technicalities but by trying to apply the "prudent person" test. Do utilize the case histories and suggestions provided in this book, of course, but when the rules cannot be stretched to fit the case, take a deep breath, step back from the situation, and use the standard of the prudent person exercising common sense.

For example, is a story news? Think of an intelligent person whom you respect and ask yourself if he or she would be interested in the story. If so, it's probably news. And if you review chapter 2 you will find that most of the suggestions posed do relate to the "prudent person" test, directly or indirectly. The same applies to decisions highlighted in other chapters.

Second, this examination of journalistic decisions seems to show that in most cases a good decision is a reasoned decision. That is, a good call is one that can be justified after the fact by logical reasoning; a good call is one that follows an organized thought process. Some decisions—including some very bad decisions—are made purely by reflex or because "we've always done it that way." But the good calls presented in this work generally had one thing in common: they were made for specific reasons, and the reporter was able, after the fact, to explain his or her reasoning.

When in doubt, ask yourself *why* (or *why not*) you intend to follow a certain path. What are the reasons? Do those reasons reflect industry standards, and do those reasons seem logical and prudent? Forcing yourself to examine your reasoning process at the very least will clarify some of the steps in the decision-making process.

The Decision-Making Process in Journalism has attempted to elucidate the reasoning process and to reinforce the idea of prudent decision-making, as well as dealing with the specifics of judging newsworthiness, truth, fairness, logic, distortion, libel, ethics, and consequences. If nothing else, we have seen that the experience of others is a good teacher. And placed in the context of a book, experience is a forgiving teacher. Perhaps you do not agree with the way some of the decisions presented in this work were made. That, of course, is your prerogative—you are free to exercise it without fear of the consequences. You may be absolutely right in your disagreement, although it is difficult to make a case for "right" or "wrong" since there are so few absolutes in journalism. The important factor is that you have exercised a few mental muscles in the decision-making process.

All journalists do this from time to time; professional journals bristle with lively debate on the tough calls. Journalists know the importance of considering the options in advance. Follow their lead. Try to plan ahead. Keep an active mind—and an open one.

REFERENCES

Adler, R. (1971). *A day in the life of the New York Times.* Philadelphia, PA: Lippincott.

Anderson, E. (1987, Summer/Autumn). How managing editors view and deal with ethical issues. *Journalism Quarterly,* pp. 341–345.

Atwater, T. (1986). Consonance in local television news. *Journal of Broadcasting and Electronic Media, 30* (4), 462–472.

Author regains rights to *Missing,* files suit for lost income and damages. (1987, Fall). *Authors Guild Bulletin,* pp. 2–3.

Award for name use stands. (1987, Winter). *Mass Media and the Law,* p. 25.

Biagi, S. (1987). *NewsTalk II: Conversations with today's broadcast journalists.* Belmont, CA: Wadsworth.

Bittner, J.R. & Bittner, D.A. (1977). *Radio journalism.* Englewood Cliffs, NJ: Prentice-Hall.

Bloch, M. (1964). *The historian's craft.* New York: Random House.

Boylan, J. (1986, December). Vietnam: The roads to Tet. *Columbia Journalism Review,* pp. 35–36.

Court denies a distress call. (1988, March 7). *Newsweek,* p. 8.

Davenport, S.D. & Izard, R.S. (1985–86). Restrictive policies of the mass media. *Journal of Mass Media Ethics, 1* (1), 4–9.

Davis, K. Personal interview. Series of interviews November 1986 through March 1987.

Engel, S.M. (1986). *With good reason: An introduction to informal fallacies.* New York: St. Martin's.

Fogelin, R. J. (1987). *Understanding arguments* (3rd ed.). Orlando, FL: Harcourt Brace Jovanovich.

Forer, L. (1987, December 14). Comments on libel laws made during interview program "Sonya Live in L.A."

Friendly, F. (1987, March 3). *The second conference on TV & ethics.* Symposium conducted by Emerson College, Boston, MA.

Garneau, G. (1989, July 1). First Amendment upheld: Supreme Court overturns lower court ruling that assessed damages against a Florida weekly for publishing a rape victim's name. *Editor & Publisher,* pp. 10, 11.

Kilpatrick, J.J. (1987, December 27). If it wasn't libel, what was it? Syndicated column, in *Worcester Telegram,* p. B–1.

Labunski, R.E. & Pavlik, J.V. (1986). The legal environment of investigative reporters: A pilot study. *Media Asia, 13* (1), 43–45.

Leslie, J. (1986, September). The anonymous source: Second thoughts on Deep Throat. *Washington Journalism Review,* pp. 33–35.

Martin, M.L. (1979). *Editing in the electronic era.* Ames, IA: Iowa State University Press.

Metzler, K. (1986). *Newsgathering* (2nd ed.). Englewood Cliffs, NJ: Prentice-Hall.

Mullen, et al. (1986). Newscaster's facial expressions and voting behaviors of viewers: Can a smile elect a president? *Journal of Personality and Social Psychology, 51* (2), 291–295.

News reporting and ethics. (1987, March 3). Panel discussion of television news directors presented as part of *Second conference on TV & ethics.* Symposium conducted by Emerson College, Boston, MA.

O'Donnell, L., Hausman, C. & Benoit, P. (1987). *Announcing: Broadcast communicating today.* Belmont, CA: Wadsworth.

Packard, V. Personal interview. (1987, August 23).

Palmer, N.D. (1987, November). Going after the truth—in disguise: The ethics of deception. *Washington Journalism Review,* pp. 20–22.

Petrow, R. Personal interview. (1987, December 3).

Radolph, A. (1987, October 10). Mounain or molehill: Six-month-old controversy over the lack of attribution in an award-winning newspaper article is still drawing opinions from editors. *Editor & Publisher,* pp. 113, 56, 60.

Rehnquist Court smiles on satire. (1988, March 7). *U.S. News & World Report,* pp. 11, 12.

Riffe D. et al. (1986). Gatekeeping and the network news mix. *Journalism Quarterly, 63* (2), 315–321.

Rottenberg, A.T. (1985). *Elements of argument: A text and reader.* New York: St. Martin's.

Sandman, P.S., Rubin, D.M. & Sachsman, D.B. (1977). *Media casebook: An introductory reader in american mass communications* (2nd ed.). Englewood Cliffs, NJ: Prentice-Hall.

Schulte, H. Personal interview. (1987, December 8).

Seeger, A. (1987, Spring). Diagrams simplify complicated issues in media law class. *Journalism Educator*, pp. 41–46.

Short, M. Personal interview and presentation. (1987, December 9).

Stein, M.L. (1987, October 24). Anonymous sources: The use of information from unnamed persons in news stories has continued to grow. *Editor & Publisher*, p. 17.

Stephens, M. (1981, July/August). "More 'Jimmy' fallout." *Washington Journalism Review*, p. 13.

Stepp, C.S. (1986, December). When a public figure's private life is news. *Washington Journalism Review*, pp. 39–41.

Swain, B.M. (1978). *Reporters' ethics.* Ames, IA: Iowa University Press.

Threat of suit silences criticism. (1985, Fall-Winter). *News Media and the Law*, p. 17.

Turk, J.V. (1986, December). Information content and media content: A study of PR influence on the news. *Journalism Monographs, 100,* 2–29.

Wallace, M., & Gates, G.P. (1984). *Close encounters.* New York: Morrow.

Whearley, J. Personal interview. (1987, November 29).

Wheeler, M. (1976). *Lies, damn lies, and statistics.* New York: Dell.

White, T., Meppen, A.J. & Young, S. (1984). *Broadcast news writing, reporting and production.* New York: Macmillan.

White, T.H. (1978). *In search of history: A personal adventure.* New York: Harper & Row.

INDEX